Practice Book

Grade 6

Harcourt School Publishers

www.harcourtschool.com

Printed in the United States of America

ISBN 10: 0-15-349880-3
ISBN 13: 978-0-15-349880-0

6 7 8 9 10 1421 17 16 15 14 13 12 11 10 09

Contents

DIVE RIGHT IN

Name _____

▶ **Which sentence makes more sense? Underline it.**

Sentence 1	Sentence 2
1. If you throw that crumpled paper against the wall, it may *ricochet* and hit Bob.	If you throw that crumpled paper at Bob, he may *ricochet* against the wall.
2. Mary was *incapacitated* for a few days because of her pretty new dress.	Mary was *incapacitated* for a few days because of her sore throat.
3. John was *crestfallen* when he won the swimming competition.	John was *crestfallen* when he lost the swimming competition.
4. The clown *lamented* when his makeup washed off in the rain.	The clown *lamented* when the children laughed at him.
5. A funny movie often causes me to scream with *mirth*.	A scary movie often causes me to scream with *mirth*.
6. I could tell he was getting *hysterical* when he began talking very softly and slowly.	I could tell he was getting *hysterical* when he began talking louder and faster.

▶ **Use what you know about the Vocabulary Words to answer the questions below. Write your answers in complete sentences.**

7. What kind of present would cause you to become *ecstatic*? _____

_____

8. What *perishable* foods do you enjoy eating most? _____

_____

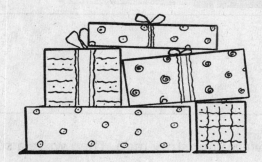

1

Name _____

▶ Read each section of "Maxx Comedy: The Funniest Kid in America." Then fill in the corresponding section of your story map.

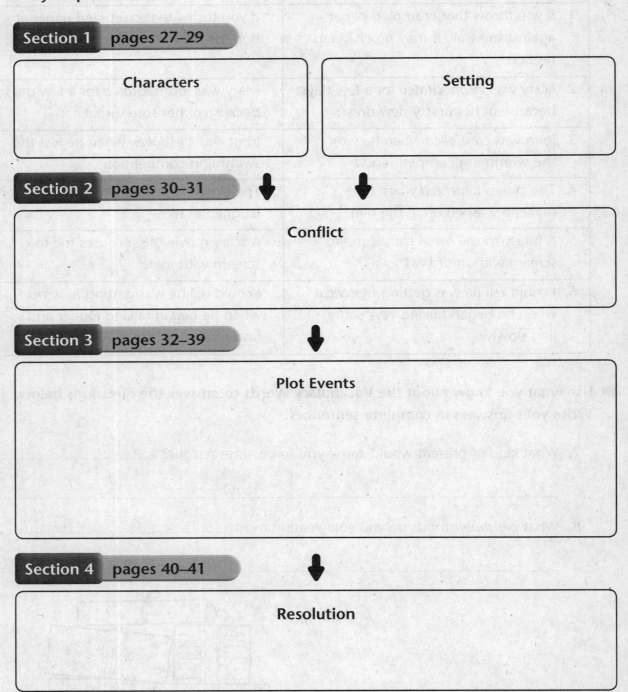

Section 1 pages 27–29

| Characters | Setting |

Section 2 pages 30–31

Conflict

Section 3 pages 32–39

Plot Events

Section 4 pages 40–41

Resolution

▶ Review your story map. Then write a summary of the selection on a separate sheet of paper.

Practice Book
© Harcourt • Grade 6

Name _____

▶ **Read the passage below. Then write your answers to the questions in the appropriate box in the story map.**

> Last week, Charles agreed to give a funny speech at a school assembly. However, he hadn't realized that Ms. Lind would want to read a complete copy of his speech the day before!
>
> The deadline passed, and Charles still didn't have his speech ready. He walked to Ms. Lind's office to apologize. Ms. Lind looked up from her desk. "How's the speech?" she asked. At that moment Charles knew that he had to tell her the truth. Ms. Lind said she would help him write the speech if he would stay after school. Charles breathed a sigh of relief and thanked her. The next day, the school auditorium roared with laughter while Charles gave his speech.

Characters	Setting

↓ ↓

Conflict

↓

Plot Events

↓

Resolution

School–Home Connection

Have your child draw a story map and explain it to you. Watch a TV program or movie together, and work together to fill in the map.

3

Practice Book
© Harcourt • Grade 6

Name _____

▶ Each sentence below describes a form of fiction. Fill in each blank to name the form.

> ### The Forms of Fiction
>
> | | | | |
> |---|---|---|---|
> | realistic fiction | fable | historical fiction | myth |
> | short story | folktale | science fiction | tall tale |

1. It is not as long as a novel and can often be read in one sitting.

   _____

2. It teaches a lesson about right and wrong and often includes talking animals.

   _____

3. It is a story that has been told in a culture for many generations.

   _____

4. It usually takes place in the future and often includes amazing inventions.

   _____

5. It is a humorous story about the adventures of an American folk hero.

   _____

▶ Read the following short paragraphs. Then fill in the blank to name the form of fiction.

6. The snake began to hiss. "I will dry out this land," he said. After many years of work, the snake had finally created Death Valley.

   This is a paragraph from _____.

7. The clouds lifted over the Great Pyramid. The workers had finally finished building it. Ra-el looked at his father and smiled.

   This paragraph is an example of _____.

8. Thomas felt great about the school play. He knew he was a very good actor and would probably get a big part. His parents and friends agreed.

   This is a paragraph of _____.

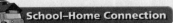
School–Home Connection

Have your child describe the different forms of fiction. Select one. Work together to create a story that your child can share with classmates.

4

Practice Book
© Harcourt • Grade 6

Name _____

▶ Fold the paper along the dotted line. As each Spelling Word
is read aloud, write it in the blank. Then unfold your paper
and check your work. Practice writing any Spelling Words
you missed.

1. _____
2. _____
3. _____
4. _____
5. _____
6. _____
7. _____
8. _____
9. _____
10. _____
11. _____
12. _____
13. _____
14. _____
15. _____
16. _____
17. _____
18. _____
19. _____
20. _____

Spelling Words

1. absences
2. against
3. album
4. circuit
5. bronze
6. chess
7. biscuit
8. depth
9. cabinet
10. drenched
11. glimpse
12. nozzle
13. feather
14. plastic
15. publish
16. pulse
17. rapid
18. snack
19. solve
20. system

School–Home Connection

Have your child write the Spelling Words and
underline the letter or letters that stand for
the short vowel sound in each word.

Practice Book
© Harcourt • Grade 6

Name _____

▶ **Add words to the following to make complete sentences. Use correct punctuation and capitalization. Then identify the type of sentence.**

1. world's largest catsup bottle in Illinois

_____

2. stand Mayor's statue

_____

3. the model of the planet Saturn

_____

4. America's Leaning Tower

_____

5. my favorite stop Metropolis, Illinois

_____

▶ **Rewrite each sentence with correct punctuation and capitalization. Underline the interjections.**

6. there is a lot of traffic ahead

_____

7. we are not on the right road

_____

8. hey, settle down in the back seat

_____

9. do you have your seat belt fastened

_____

10. Wow, the view is beautiful

_____

School–Home Connection

Ask your child to draw a four-column chart. Label the columns "declarative," "interrogative," "imperative," and "exclamatory." Ask him or her to write two example sentences in each column.

6

Name _____

▶ **Which example is better? Underline the sentence.**

Word	Sentence 1	Sentence 2
1. survey	A man peers out of his second-floor window and looks over the neighborhood.	A man goes to his second-floor bedroom and lies on his bed.
2. hovered	A butterfly zoomed quickly through the yard on its way to a flower.	A butterfly seemed to hang in the air while it drank from a flower.
3. meandering	A stream has a lot of gentle twists and turns.	A flowing river rushes toward a waterfall.
4. frolicked	The children laughed as they played tag on the field.	The children played a serious game of baseball on the field.
5. inquired	A student understood the directions for the homework assignment.	A student asked her teacher questions about the homework assignment.
6. emerged	The bear slowly crept out from the cave.	The bear slowly crept into the cave.
7. tormented	She was really bothered by all the loud noise.	She was excited when she heard all the noise.
8. subtle	The changes in her style were obvious.	You could barely notice the changes in her style.

School–Home Connection

With your child, discuss the Vocabulary Words. Have your child explain the meaning of each one. Then ask him or her to think of two good examples for each word.

Practice Book
© Harcourt • Grade 6

▶ **Read "The Color of My Words." Then complete the story map.**

```
┌──────────────────────────┐      ┌──────────────────────────┐
│      Characters          │      │       Setting            │
│                          │      │                          │
│                          │      │                          │
│                          │      │                          │
│                          │      │                          │
└──────────────────────────┘      └──────────────────────────┘
            ↓                                   ↓
┌─────────────────────────────────────────────────────────────┐
│                         Conflict                              │
│                                                               │
│                                                               │
└─────────────────────────────────────────────────────────────┘
                                ↓
┌─────────────────────────────────────────────────────────────┐
│                       Plot Events                             │
│                                                               │
│                                                               │
│                                                               │
│                                                               │
│                                                               │
└─────────────────────────────────────────────────────────────┘
                                ↓
┌─────────────────────────────────────────────────────────────┐
│                       Resolution                              │
│                                                               │
│                                                               │
│                                                               │
└─────────────────────────────────────────────────────────────┘
```

▶ **Review your story map. Then, on a separate sheet of paper, write a summary of the selection.**

8

Name _____

▶ **Read the paragraph below. Then answer the questions.**

Sharonda checked the time on her watch. It was almost five. She and her puppy Patches would really have to hurry back home from the park. They had to be home when Sharonda's cousin Laurie arrived. Laurie and her parents were coming to California for Thanksgiving and staying for a few days. Sharonda and Laurie had very different personalities and had had problems getting along in the past. However, Sharonda's parents had made her promise to be easygoing. Sharonda jogged home and got there just in time to see Laurie and her parents ring the doorbell. Since Patches liked everyone, he approached Laurie playfully and licked her hand. Laurie yanked her hand away, turned to Sharonda, and said, "I hope this isn't your mutt. I'm allergic."

1. What are the names of the characters?

_____

2. What is the main conflict in this story?

_____

_____

3. What event in the rising action makes the conflict worse?

_____

_____

4. How might the setting make the conflict worse?

_____

_____

5. What do you think will be the resolution to the conflict?

_____

_____

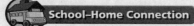

School–Home Connection

Have your child explain rising action to you.
Watch a TV program together and work as a
team to identify the events of the rising action.

9

Name _____

▶ **Fill in the blank with the name of the correct poetic device.**

rhyme	rhythm	punctuation	onomatopoeia
word choice	repetition	alliteration	

1. The same beginning sound is repeated. _____

2. The poet uses periods, question marks, or exclamation marks at the ends of sentences. _____

3. Every other line of a poem ends with a word that has the same final sound. _____

4. The poet uses vivid sensory words to describe a scene. _____

5. The poet uses the same word three times in a row. _____

6. The word imitates a sound. _____

▶ **Pretend you are a poet! Follow each direction below. Write your answers on the blanks.**

7. Write two words that rhyme with *day*.

_____

8. Make up a line of poetry that repeats the word *when*.

_____

9. Choose two vivid words to describe the sun.

_____

10. Write a line that uses the same rhythm as "I had a funny dream last night."

_____

School–Home Connection

Have your child select a poem from a book or magazine and read it to you. Then discuss the poet's use of poetic devices.

10

Name _____

▶ Fold the paper along the dotted line. As each Spelling Word is read aloud, write it in the blank. Then unfold your paper and check your work. Practice writing any Spelling Words you missed.

1. _____
2. _____
3. _____
4. _____
5. _____
6. _____
7. _____
8. _____
9. _____
10. _____
11. _____
12. _____
13. _____
14. _____
15. _____
16. _____
17. _____
18. _____
19. _____
20. _____

Spelling Words

1. sneeze
2. arcade
3. vacuum
4. breathe
5. belief
6. proclaim
7. entertain
8. quaint
9. aglow
10. saying
11. essay
12. tomorrow
13. coffee
14. stride
15. easel
16. approach
17. globe
18. polite
19. duty
20. grief

 School–Home Connection

Work with your child to write a sentence for each Spelling Word. Have your child circle the vowel pairs in each Spelling Word that make the long vowel sound.

11

Name _____

▶ Complete each sentence with one of the simple subjects or
simple predicates in the box.

Simple Subjects			
seagulls	people	Kim	sister
Simple Predicates			
crash	takes		look

1. _____ enjoys swimming in the ocean.

2. The _____ swoop down for food.

3. My little _____ digs a hole in the sand.

4. The waves _____ on the beach.

5. My aunt always _____ an umbrella to the beach.

6. Many _____ forget sunscreen.

7. _____ at the dolphins.

▶ Write complete sentences by adding complete subjects or complete predicates
or both.

8. friend Susan

_____

9. read stories

_____

10. have surprise endings

_____

School–Home Connection

Ask your child to write a paragraph about a
recent family holiday or event. Then ask him or
her to underline the simple subjects and circle
the simple predicates.

12

Name _____

▶ **Write the Vocabulary Word that matches each definition.**

> schemes   exerts   rigged   astounding
> replica   stabilize   disbanded

1. _____ very surprising

2. _____ stopped operating as a group

3. _____ a copy or model

4. _____ plans for getting something you want

5. _____ uses physical effort

6. _____ to make something less likely to break or topple over

7. _____ made something with available materials

▶ **Use what you know about the Vocabulary Words to respond to the items below. Write complete sentences.**

8. If your baseball team *disbanded,* what would you do?

_____

9. Describe the expression on your face when you see something *astounding.*

_____

10. Would you want to climb a ladder that was not *stabilized*? Why or why not?

_____

School–Home Connection

With your child, discuss the meaning of the
Vocabulary Words. Work together to think
of a sentence you might use in everyday
conversation for each Vocabulary Word.

13

Name _____

▶ Read each section of "The Wright Brothers: A Flying Start."
Then answer the questions in the chart.

Section 1 pages 84–89

When and why did Orville and Wilbur first decide to build a flying machine?

_____

_____

_____

⬇

Section 2 pages 90–93

What did the Wright Brothers build in 1900? What important information did they learn in 1901?

_____

_____

⬇

Section 3 pages 94–97

What happened on December 17, 1903?

_____

_____

⬇

Section 4 pages 98–101

When did people finally recognize what the Wright brothers had accomplished?

_____

_____

▶ Use the information in the chart to write a summary of the selection.

14

Name _____

▶ Read the paragraph below. Then figure out the correct chronological order for the five statements. In the sequence chart, write the letters of the statements in correct chronological order.

> In 1593, doctors did not yet understand what the heart did or how blood circulated throughout the body. That year a teenager named William Harvey began studying medicine in England. He settled in London as a doctor in 1602. Seven years later, he was appointed to an important post at the only hospital in London. Harvey always felt that his education about the heart had not been correct. So in 1610 he began conducting research on animals. For eighteen years he studied the heart, the lungs, and the route that blood takes through animals' bodies. In 1628, he published a book called *The Motion of the Heart and Blood in Animals*. Later, his discoveries were shown to apply to humans too.

A. William Harvey's discoveries were proved to apply to humans.

B. William Harvey settled in London as a doctor.

C. William Harvey began conducting research on animals.

D. William Harvey began studying medicine.

E. William Harvey was appointed to an important post in a London hospital.

1. First	2. Next	3. Then	4. Next	5. Finally
_____	_____	_____	_____	_____

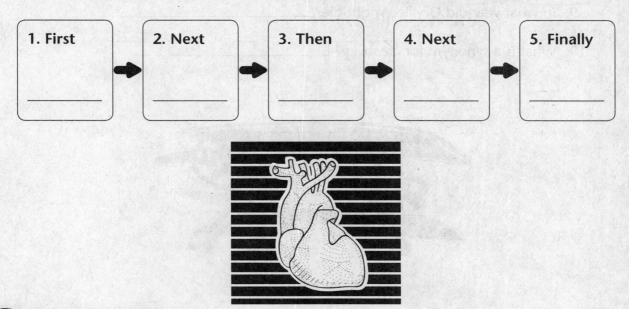

School–Home Connection

Work with your child to list eight events that happen every weekday in your home. Have your child create a sequence chart and fill it in with these events.

15

Name _____

▶ You can save time doing research if you know which reference source is most likely to contain the information you need. Read each question below. Then choose the reference source that is most likely to answer the question.

> almanac   atlas   dictionary
> encyclopedia   thesaurus

1. Where is England in relation to France? _____

2. How do you pronounce the word *scheme*? _____

3. What were the earliest bicycles like? _____

4. What are the world's three highest mountains? _____

5. What word means the opposite of *stabilize*? _____

6. What is the definition of *replica*? _____

7. How far apart are Ohio and North Carolina? _____

8. What is the world's fastest airplane? _____

9. In what year did Orville Wright die? _____

10. What is a synonym for *creativity*? _____

School–Home Connection

Work together with your child to write five questions to research. Have your child select appropriate reference sources at home or at school and use them to answer the questions.

16

Name _____

▶ Fold the paper along the dotted line. As each Spelling Word is read aloud, write it in the blank. Then unfold your paper and check your work. Practice writing any Spelling Words you missed.

1. _____
2. _____
3. _____
4. _____
5. _____
6. _____
7. _____
8. _____
9. _____
10. _____
11. _____
12. _____
13. _____
14. _____
15. _____
16. _____
17. _____
18. _____
19. _____
20. _____

Spelling Words

1. authentic
2. launch
3. boycott
4. turquoise
5. withdrawn
6. awkward
7. faulty
8. applaud
9. jigsaw
10. curfew
11. pound
12. awesome
13. corduroy
14. shrewd
15. soothing
16. booklet
17. drowsy
18. moisture
19. flaunt
20. ointment

School–Home Connection

Have your child write the Spelling Words in alphabetical order. Then have him or her write them in reverse alphabetical order.

17

Name _____

▶ **Underline the compound subject or compound predicate.
Then circle the conjunction.**

1. Airplanes and ships carry passengers over long distances.

2. John rides his bicycle or walks to school.

3. The driver fastens her seat belt, checks her mirrors, and starts the car.

4. Buses, trucks, and cars filled the parking lot.

▶ **Combine each pair of sentences to make one sentence with a compound subject or
a compound predicate.**

5. My sister wants a new bicycle. I want a new bicycle.

   _____

6. A bicycle has two wheels. A bicycle is steered with handlebars.

   _____

7. Adults enjoy riding bicycles. Children enjoy riding bicycles.

   _____

8. Ten-speed bikes have multiple gears. Twelve-speed bikes have multiple gears.

   _____

9. Three-speed bikes are heavy. Three-speed bikes do not go very fast.

   _____

10. Michael has a BMX bike. Keyshawn has a BMX bike.

    _____

School–Home Connection

Ask your child to write sentences about a family
outing. Help him or her write simple sentences
describing what family members did at the
event. Ask your child to identify compound
subjects and predicates in sentences.

18

Name _____

▶ Which sentence makes more sense? Underline that sentence.

Word	Sentence 1	Sentence 2
1. fumble	After my *fumble*, my mom said I must have put butter on my fingers.	After my *fumble*, my mom told everyone I made a great play.
2. astonishment	We looked in *astonishment* as the traffic light turned green.	We looked in *astonishment* at the huge flock of birds flying overhead.
3. remedies	My grandma used old-fashioned *remedies* for curing a cold.	My grandma used old-fashioned *remedies* for making soup.
4. luxury	It was a *luxury* to eat in the fancy restaurant.	It was a *luxury* to have dinner around the kitchen table.
5. triumphant	Forgetting my lunch on the bus was a *triumphant* moment.	Reaching my goal of twenty sit-ups was a *triumphant* moment.
6. lunged	The gardener *lunged* at a bed of flowers and picked a bouquet.	The gardener *lunged* at a rabbit that was eating his vegetables.

▶ Use what you know about the Vocabulary Words to answer the questions below. Write complete sentences.

7. What would you do if the race was too *intense* for you to watch?

_____

_____

8. Would you use a rope or a pair of oars to *propel* a boat through the water? Why?

_____

_____

School–Home Connection

With your child, discuss the Vocabulary Words. Have your child tell you what each one means. Ask your child to think of two sentences using each word.

19

Practice Book
© Harcourt • Grade 6

► Read "Wilma Unlimited." Then write the major events from Wilma Rudolph's life in chronological order.

```
┌─────────────────────────────────┐
│                                 │
└─────────────────────────────────┘
              ↓
┌─────────────────────────────────┐
│                                 │
└─────────────────────────────────┘
              ↓
┌─────────────────────────────────┐
│                                 │
└─────────────────────────────────┘
              ↓
┌─────────────────────────────────┐
│                                 │
└─────────────────────────────────┘
              ↓
┌─────────────────────────────────┐
│                                 │
└─────────────────────────────────┘
```

► Think about the information on the chart. Then, on a separate sheet of paper, write a summary of the selection.

Name _____

▶ **Read the passage below. Then write the events in the sequence chart in the correct order. Underline the word or words that indicate the sequence.**

The first Olympic Games were held in ancient Greece in 776 B.C. It was a time for the warring city-states to put down their weapons and compete in peace. The Games were played every four years, until A.D. 393.

In 1893, Pierre de Coubertin decided the world again needed the Olympic Games. He believed games such as the Olympics would encourage peace and goodwill. One year later, delegates met in Paris to discuss Pierre's idea. They voted for the first modern Olympics to be held in Athens in 1896, and the Olympics have been held every four years since. Today, the Olympics still stand for peace and goodwill among nations.

- One year later, delegates met in Paris to discuss Pierre's idea.
- In 1893, Pierre de Coubertin decided the world again needed the Olympic Games.
- The first Olympic Games were held in ancient Greece in 776 B.C.
- Today, the Olympics stand for peace and goodwill among nations.
- The Olympic Games were played every four years, until A.D. 393.

1. [   ]

⬇

2. [   ]

⬇

3. [   ]

⬇

4. [   ]

⬇

5. [   ]

School–Home Connection

Work with your child to list six events that have occurred in his or her life. Have your child fill in a sequence chart to show the order of the events.

Practice Book
© Harcourt • Grade 6

Name _____

▶ **Fold the paper along the dotted line. As each Spelling Word is read aloud, write it in the blank. Then unfold your paper and check your work. Practice writing any Spelling Words you missed.**

1. _____

2. _____

3. _____

4. _____

5. _____

6. _____

7. _____

8. _____

9. _____

10. _____

11. _____

12. _____

13. _____

14. _____

15. _____

16. _____

17. _____

18. _____

19. _____

20. _____

Spelling Words

1. decorating
2. applying
3. delaying
4. employed
5. studying
6. supposed
7. exciting
8. married
9. envied
10. studied
11. frightened
12. panicked
13. relayed
14. preparing
15. replied
16. invited
17. multiplied
18. planning
19. lying
20. served

School–Home Connection

Work with your child to write the base word for each Spelling Word. For example, the base word for *replied* is *reply*.

22

Practice Book

Name _____

▶ **Rewrite each sentence with a correct coordinating conjunction.**

1. Mary McLeod Bethune was born in South Carolina she later moved to Florida.

   _____

2. Bethune went to college she had to work, too.

   _____

3. She worked as a teacher she traveled throughout the South.

   _____

4. Bethune was president of a college she was active in politics.

   _____

5. Bethune was a community leader, she advised Presidents.

   _____

▶ **Rewrite each compound sentence to make two simple sentences.**

6. The U.S. Supreme Court made segregation illegal in 1954; the court case was Brown v. Board of Education.

   _____

   _____

7. The bus boycott was a success, and Rosa Parks had sparked it.

   _____

8. Many people joined the protest, and the boycott lasted from 1955 to 1956.

   _____

School–Home Connection

Ask your child to write a paragraph about a topic of his or her choice. It should include simple and compound sentences. Ask your child to underline the compound sentences and circle the conjunctions.

23

Read the first version of the story. In the second version, replace the underlined words with Vocabulary Words from the box. Use each Vocabulary Word only once.

intimidating	calamity	invaluable	quandary
composure	hindrance	steadfast	surpassed
	sage	trepidation	

Version 1

It was just before curtain time, and I was in a <u>dilemma</u> about what to do. The news crew would be here soon, and a <u>terrible event</u> was about to happen. It was a <u>frightening</u> situation. Dr. Preston had called in sick and couldn't do the interview. Where could I find another <u>priceless</u> <u>wise person</u> like Dr. Preston? Who could have just as much <u>coolness under pressure</u>? It could only be my friend Molly Krell, a professor.

Dr. Krell is <u>firm</u> in her beliefs. She knows who she is, what she wants, and where she's going. There was no sign of <u>fear</u> on her part. Dr. Preston's cancellation was a minor <u>difficulty</u> as far as she was concerned. Dr. Krell did the interview and <u>went beyond</u> my expectations!

Version 2

It was just before curtain time, and I was in a _____ about what to do. The news crew would be here soon, and a _____ was about to happen. It was a(n) _____ situation. Dr. Preston had called in sick and couldn't do the interview. Where could I find another _____ like Dr. Preston? Who could have just as much _____? It could only be my friend Molly Krell, a professor.

Dr. Krell is _____ in her beliefs. She knows who she is, what she wants, and where she's going. There was no sign of _____ on her part. Dr. Preston's cancellation was a minor _____ as far as she was concerned. Dr. Krell did the interview and _____ my expectations!

Practice Book
© Harcourt • Grade 6

Name _____

▶ **Read the story below. Then use complete sentences to answer the questions that follow.**

> Elvin walked slowly home from school one day. Tryouts for the school basketball team were going to take place the next night. Elvin wanted badly to try out, but he also had band practice the next night. It was required practice. The band would be marching in a parade on Saturday, and members needed to get the formation just right. Elvin loved being in the band and marching, but he also loved basketball. How could he try out and not miss practice?
>
> Later that evening Elvin sat in his clubhouse with his three best friends. They were all trying to figure out what Elvin could do to solve his problem. One suggested he talk to his band director and see if he could be late to practice. Another suggested he talk to the basketball coach and ask to try out earlier than the rest of the players. Still another suggested Elvin quit band and only concentrate on playing basketball this year. Elvin didn't know what to do. He loved both, but did he have to choose one over the other?

1. Where does the first part of this story take place?

_____

_____

2. What problem does Elvin have?

_____

_____

3. Whom does Elvin go to for help?

_____

_____

4. What is the setting in the second paragraph of the story?

_____

_____

5. What solutions do Elvin's friends come up with for his problem?

_____

_____

School–Home Connection

Your child is reviewing plot and setting. Have your child read the story above and his or her answers to the questions. Then have your child choose among the suggestions for how Elvin might solve his problem.

25

Practice Book
© Harcourt • Grade 6

▶ **Read the passage below. Use complete sentences to answer the questions that follow.**

Mysterious Light over City

CHICAGO—A strange glow was seen over the city last night. It hovered for about five minutes and then disappeared. Reports are scattered about the glow and its origin, but some people said that it came from the East as a small point of light traveling fast. Many thought it was a shooting star or a meteor. The glow grew larger and larger until it practically covered the downtown area. When the glow hovered, it shed light on the entire lakefront. Traffic stopped. Night turned into day, and a few brave souls ventured outside. Some said that the light gave them a sense of warmth and a feeling of joy. Others said it felt as if the sun had come back out. Then the light rose into the sky and disappeared, bringing back night. For a moment, the whole city seemed eerily quiet. Then traffic started flowing again, and the city noises returned. Just what the light was and what effect it may have on the future are unsolved mysteries.

1. What happened first with the strange light?

_____

2. Once the light reached downtown Chicago, what did it do?

_____

_____

3. What happened while the light hovered over the city?

_____

_____

4. What happened to the light after five minutes?

_____

_____

5. What happened last?

_____

_____

School–Home Connection

Your child is reviewing chronological order.
Review the answers your child gave and
have him or her find chronological order in
newspaper articles.

26

Practice Book
© Harcourt • Grade 6

Name _____

▶ Read each passage. Identify the form of fiction it shows. Then give the passage a title that reflects that form.

> Father and I are planning to go the public baths today. The public baths offer a place to cool off and learn what is going on in the Senate. I learn so much about politics and the running of a large city like Rome. I especially like when the men discuss Caesar. Father once let me go down to the stables and look at his chariot and horses. It is always a grand time there.

1. Form of Fiction: _____

2. Possible Title: _____

> The pony named Edgar neighed, recognizing Jamie as she approached his stall. It had been a while since she had ridden her favorite pony. Edgar nudged Jamie's hand, looking for the carrot she always brought him on her visits. The pony wasn't disappointed as Jamie opened her palm. While Edgar ate, Jamie rubbed his mane and talked to him gently. She apologized for not visiting for so long. Then she found the saddle and bridle. She'd ride Edgar today—she needed to feel the wind on her face.

3. Form of Fiction: _____

4. Possible Title: _____

> "Doesn't Earth look lovely tonight?" Carlo asked his wife.
> "Yes, dear," she replied. "It gives off a wonderful blue glow in the night sky."
> "We must go visit your mother soon," Carlo said. "Space travel is just too much for her, and it's been a while since she's seen the children. They'd love to hear the stories she tells about the great flood of 2121."
> Carlo's wife nodded. "It's also been some time since I've been to my childhood home on Earth. My old high school is planning a reunion this year. It would be nice to see old friends again. Let's plan our visit around that."
> Carlo nodded. "Yes. Let's plan a trip home."

5. Form of Fiction: _____

6. Possible Title: _____

School–Home Connection

Your child is reviewing forms of fiction. Have your child identify different forms of fiction in reading materials around the house.

27

Read the entries below from reference sources. Then use complete sentences to answer the questions.

Dictionary Entry

fountain (foun´tən) n. 1. flow of water rising into the air in a spray. 2. spring or source of water. 3. place to get a drink: *water fountain*. [Old French *fontaine*; Latin *fontāna*, of a spring]

Thesaurus Entry

imperfect *adj.* deficient, defective, faulty, blemished, flawed, marred, unfinished, undeveloped, below par. *Antonyms* perfect, absolute, ideal, utopian, flawless, unmarred.

Almanac Entry

Population Explosion Among Older Americans: The United States saw a rapid growth in its elderly population during the 20th century. The number of Americans age 65 and older climbed above 34.9 million in 2000, compared with 3.1 million in 1900. For the same years, the ratio of elderly Americans to the total population jumped from 1 in 25 to 1 in 8. The trend is guaranteed to continue in the next century as the baby-boom generation ages. Between 1990 and 2020, the population age 65 to 74 is projected to grow 74%.

Source: Based on U.S. Census Bureau data

1. How many definitions are given for *fountain*?

   _____

2. What part of speech is *fountain*?

   _____

3. From what Old French word is *fountain* derived?

   _____

4. What are three synonyms for *imperfect*?

   _____

5. What are three antonyms for *imperfect*?

   _____

6. How fast is the elderly population projected to grow between 1990 and 2020?

   _____

Practice Book
© Harcourt • Grade 6

Name _____

▶ Fold the paper along the dotted line. As each Spelling Word is read aloud, write it in the blank. Then unfold your paper and check your work. Practice writing any Spelling Words you missed.

1. _____
2. _____
3. _____
4. _____
5. _____
6. _____
7. _____
8. _____
9. _____
10. _____
11. _____
12. _____
13. _____
14. _____
15. _____
16. _____
17. _____
18. _____
19. _____
20. _____

Spelling Words

1. circuit
2. against
3. cabinet
4. feather
5. system
6. sneeze
7. proclaim
8. grief
9. approach
10. arcade
11. aglow
12. breathe
13. pound
14. applaud
15. turquoise
16. awkward
17. delaying
18. employed
19. replied
20. preparing

29

Name _____

▶ **Read this part of a student's rough draft. Then answer the questions that follow.**

> (1) Who inspired the talk shows of today? (2) Phil Donahue inspired them (3) He heard his voice on a college radio station. (4) He was instantly hooked on radio. (5) Later he worked in radio as an announcer, news director, and morning newscaster. (6) A TV talk show hired him as the host in 1967.

1. Which type of sentence is Sentence 1?
   A declarative
   B imperative
   C exclamatory
   D interrogative

2. Which sentence is missing an end mark?
   A Sentence 1
   B Sentence 2
   C Sentence 3
   D Sentence 4

3. Which type of sentence is Sentence 4?
   A declarative
   B imperative
   C exclamatory
   D interrogative

4. Which is the complete subject of Sentence 6?
   A A TV talk show
   B A TV
   C talk show
   D show

5. Which is the simple predicate of Sentence 5?
   A as the host
   B as an announcer, news director, and morning newscaster
   C worked
   D worked in radio

6. Which is the complete predicate of Sentence 3?
   A heard
   B heard his voice
   C heard his voice on a college radio station
   D voice on a college radio station

▶ **Read this part of a student's rough draft. Then answer the questions that follow.**

> (1) Television became a part of Americans' lives after World War II when the first large TV audience watched the World Series of 1947. (2) TV producers and script writers learned what people liked through trial and error. (3) *Milton Berle's Texaco Star Theater* was a popular show. (4) *Milton Berle's Texaco Star Theater* had many acts. (5) Today three of the first networks are popular and still operate. (6) Competition for viewers is more fierce than ever.

1. Which two sentences have the same subject and can be rewritten as one sentence?
   - A Sentences 1 and 2
   - B Sentences 3 and 4
   - C Sentences 4 and 5
   - D Sentences 5 and 6

2. Which sentence has a compound subject?
   - A Sentence 1
   - B Sentence 2
   - C Sentence 3
   - D Sentence 5

3. Which sentence has a compound predicate?
   - A Sentence 3
   - B Sentence 4
   - C Sentence 5
   - D Sentence 6

4. Which of the following sentences is a run-on?
   - A Sentence 1
   - B Sentence 2
   - C Sentence 3
   - D Sentence 4

5. Which of the following terms best describes Sentence 2?
   - A compound
   - B simple
   - C run-on
   - D comma splice

6. Which is the correct way to combine Sentences 5 and 6?
   - A , but
   - B ,
   - C , or,
   - D ; with

31

Name _____

▶ **Which sentence makes more sense? Underline it.**

Sentence 1	Sentence 2
1. The woman was cautious while driving on the *sinuous* mountain roads.	The woman sped up while driving on the *sinuous* mountain roads.
2. Jim found it difficult to touch his toes because he was so *supple*.	Jim found it easy to touch his toes because he was so *supple*.
3. During the electrical storm, the television went *haywire*.	After I turned it off, the television went *haywire*.
4. I can always tell when Dad is speaking in *jest*, because his voice is so loud.	I can always tell when Dad is speaking in *jest*, because of the twinkle in his eyes.

▶ **Use what you know about the Vocabulary Words to answer the questions below. Write your answers in complete sentences.**

5. How would you *fuse* together two broken pieces of a candle? _____

_____

6. How do you change the *intonation* of your voice to show that you are asking a

question? _____

_____

7. Is a statue made of bronze or a statue made of plastic more likely to be *immobile*?

Explain. _____

_____

School–Home Connection

With your child, discuss the Vocabulary Words. Have your child tell you the meaning of each word in his or her own words. Encourage your child to use each word in a sentence.

32

▶ As you read "Befiddled," answer the questions below to fill in the story map.

Characters
How is Mr. Freeman different from Becky?

Setting
Where does the story take place?

Conflict
What conflict does Mr. Freeman see within Becky?

Plot Events
What does Mr. Freeman do to help Becky solve her problem?

Resolution
How does Becky resolve her conflict?

▶ Use the information in your story map to write a summary on a separate sheet of paper.

▶ **Read the story below. Then fill in the story map.**

> Brian could make anybody laugh—especially his best friend, Zach. The boys were waiting to try out for the lead in the school play. Zach was really nervous.
>
> "Zach, don't be shy. Stand up and let them see what you've got!" (Zach, who was short and very sensitive about it, was already standing up.) Zach grew very quiet, but Brian continued, "You shouldn't let things get you down. That's the long and the short of it." Zach sighed and walked away.
>
> "I really blew it," Brian thought. He talked to Ms. Abel, the director of the play.
>
> "Hi, Zach!" he said. "I'm sorry about my lame jokes. Guess what? Ms. Abel needs a great reader like you to be the narrator for the play. She said she'd like for you to try out today." Zach's big smile was as sweet as applause to Brian.

Characters' Qualities	Setting

Conflict

Plot Events

Resolution

🚒 **School–Home Connection**

Talk with your child about a story you have both read. Describe the main character's qualities and tell one way these traits affected what happened in the story.

34

► Read each sentence in column 1. Match the italicized word
with the correct definition in column 2.

_____ 1. That note sounded *flat*.	A. having lost its air
_____ 2. The car had a *flat* tire.	B. below the proper pitch
_____ 3. The dog lay *flat* on its back.	C. stretched out horizontally
_____ 4. The bank charged a *flat* rate.	D. fixed; not changing
_____ 5. The lawyer won her *case*.	E. a box for holding an object
_____ 6. The detective solved the *case*.	F. an action taken in court
_____ 7. Put your violin in its *case*.	G. a particular instance or example
_____ 8. In *case* of fire, use the stairs.	H. a situation calling for investigation

► Read the sentences. Circle the letter of the meaning that fits the context for the
italicized word.

9. The injured player *ground* her teeth in pain but did not cry out.

   A   wore down by friction   C   a basis for a belief or action

   B   the surface of the earth   D   pressed together with a scraping motion

10. The teacher will *address* the class about rules for the field trip.

    A   speak to   C   direct or send

    B   a speech   D   a location or place

11. We tried to *stall* him so that he wouldn't arrive early for his surprise party.

    A   a booth   C   delay

    B   a compartment   D   break down

12. The tired children did not *object* when they were told to go to bed.

    A   complain   C   article

    B   purpose   D   target

School–Home Connection

With your child, discuss the meanings for
ground, *address*, *stall*, and *object* in the
sentences shown. Then help your child write
another sentence for each word, using one of
the other meanings.

35

Practice Book
© Harcourt • Grade 6

Name _____

▶ Fold the paper along the dotted line. As each Spelling Word
is read aloud, write it in the blank. Then unfold your paper
and check your work. Practice writing any Spelling Words
you missed.

1. _____

2. _____

3. _____

4. _____

5. _____

6. _____

7. _____

8. _____

9. _____

10. _____

11. _____

12. _____

13. _____

14. _____

15. _____

16. _____

17. _____

18. _____

19. _____

20. _____

Spelling Words

1. dangle
2. mangle
3. feeble
4. crinkle
5. wobble
6. frazzle
7. obstacle
8. tickle
9. muffle
10. bridle
11. jumble
12. kindle
13. dwindle
14. swindle
15. assemble
16. mantle
17. brittle
18. freckle
19. muzzle
20. cuticle

School–Home Connection

Have your child write the Spelling Words two
times. Then cut and separate the words. Turn
the words face down and play a matching
game together.

Name _____

▶ **Complete each sentence. Then label what you wrote as a**
prepositional phrase, preposition, **or** *object.*

1. Musical theater combines story, song, and dance _____ one stage.

   _____

2. The plot _____ a musical is simple. _____

3. Many musicals end _____. _____

4. Musicals are often based _____ books or historical events.

   _____

5. Many people enjoy seeing a show with their _____. _____

▶ **Rewrite each sentence by adding a prepositional phrase. Use the words in**
parentheses ( ) in the phrase.

6. I listen. (concert)

   _____

7. The symphony plays. (fireworks)

   _____

8. The city broadcast the symphony. (radio)

   _____

9. We stayed. (end)

   _____

10. Let's move. (stage)

    _____

School–Home Connection

Work with your child to write a list of steps
that tell how to make his or her favorite dish.
Have your child underline all the prepositional
phrases in the sentences.

37

Name _____

▶ Read the sentences. Then write the Vocabulary
Word that best completes each sentence.

ordinary	suit	treason	convince
rejected	disown	defeatist	

It was no (1) _____ day. Our team had to (2) _____

Coach Bensen to let us play one more game. He had (3) _____ our earlier

plea. It just didn't (4) _____ his purpose to have us play anymore. We had

played so badly the day before that we thought he might (5) _____ us. His

rejection felt like (6) _____, I thought, because we were the school

team. We had to stop our (7) _____ attitude and start winning.

▶ Write the next paragraph in the story above. Use at least four of
the Vocabulary Words in your paragraph.

_____

_____

_____

_____

_____

School–Home Connection

Students can keep track of where they
encounter this week's Vocabulary Words by
making a chart and writing in it the word and
the place where they heard or read it.

38

Read "S.O.R. Losers." Then answer the questions in the
story map.

Characters
Who are the main characters?
What are their qualities?

Setting
Where does this story take place?
Why?

Conflict
What conflict do the South Orange River soccer players have?

Plot Events
What are the main events of the story?

Resolution
How do the South Orange River soccer players resolve their conflict?

Use the information in your story map to write a summary of the selection on a
separate sheet of paper.

Practice Book
© Harcourt • Grade 6

▶ **Read the passages below. Then answer the questions.**

Passage 1

> Mei and her family moved recently so that her dad could get a better job. It hasn't been easy for her to make new friends. Though Mei enjoys being around people, actually getting to know them is hard. She was active in clubs and sports at her old school; she had a lot of friends there. She misses going to the movies, attending sporting events, and talking with them. Mei wants to make friends at her new school.

1. What is the conflict in this paragraph? _____

_____

2. How can Mei's qualities help solve her problem? _____

_____

Passage 2

> Calvin loves music. He took piano lessons in first and second grades, and in third grade he took trumpet lessons. He played with a borrowed instrument until his parents bought him a trumpet of his own. Calvin has been playing in his school's band for the past two years. Now in sixth grade, he wants to join the orchestra. His parents expect him to continue with the trumpet, but Calvin is tired of that instrument and is ready to try the viola.

3. What kind of person is Calvin? _____

_____

4. What is Calvin's conflict? _____

_____

_____

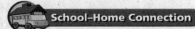

School–Home Connection

Work with your child to write a resolution for
Passage 2. Tell him or her to think about how
the character's qualities will affect the outcome.

Practice Book
© Harcourt • Grade 6

▶ **Decide which word best completes the sentence. Write it on the line. Use a dictionary if you need help.**

1. Neighbors were annoyed by Josh's _____ radio. (blaring, loud)

2. The _____ building downtown is one of the biggest in the state. (large, humongous)

3. Because I was _____, I couldn't go to school today. (diseased, sick)

4. Even though he went _____, Roger had a great time at the dance. (alone, isolated)

5. Lauren _____ her arm when she fell off her bike. (broke, destroyed)

6. Kelsey does not ride roller coasters because she is _____ of heights. (alarmed, afraid)

7. The earthquake caused the whole house to _____. (shake, shiver)

▶ **Write sentences using the words above that did not fit in the sentences. Make sure your sentences show what the words mean.**

_____

_____

_____

_____

_____

_____

_____

School–Home Connection

Have your child read aloud the new sentences.
Have him or her tell how the meanings of the
words in each pair above differ.

41

Name _____

▶ Fold the paper along the dotted line. As each Spelling Word is read aloud, write it in the blank. Then unfold your paper and check your work. Practice writing any Spelling Words you missed.

1. _____
2. _____
3. _____
4. _____
5. _____
6. _____
7. _____
8. _____
9. _____
10. _____
11. _____
12. _____
13. _____
14. _____
15. _____
16. _____
17. _____
18. _____
19. _____
20. _____

Spelling Words

1. pattern
2. associate
3. exhale
4. bulletin
5. collapse
6. complaint
7. instance
8. dessert
9. difficulty
10. franchise
11. emphasize
12. exclude
13. disturb
14. mammoth
15. necessary
16. impact
17. splendid
18. stampede
19. survival
20. wander

School–Home Connection

Work with your child to sort the Spelling Words into categories, such as Words with Double Letters or Words with the Same Vowel Sound.

42

Name _____

▶ **Underline each dependent clause and circle each
subordinating conjunction.**

1. A basketball game starts with a jump ball, when each of two opposing players tries
to tap the ball to a teammate.

2. When the home team fouled, we got to shoot free throws.

3. Although Jessica is usually a good shooter, she missed this time.

4. A game, when it is played in the NBA, has 48 minutes of playing time.

5. Because basketball is such a popular sport, it is difficult to get tickets to a game.

▶ **Write each pair of sentences as one complex sentence, using a subordinating
conjunction. Add commas where needed.**

6. Our player was out of bounds. The other team put the ball back in play.

   _____

7. The ball went into the basket and bounced out. We did not score.

   _____

8. Kelly is small. She is a very strong player.

   _____

9. This is an important game. We will try to play our best.

   _____

10. Both teams had the same score. At the end the game went into overtime.

   _____

School–Home Connection

Work with your child to write a letter to his or
her teacher describing something enjoyable
that he or she did in class. Hint: use the words
when, because, before, after, or *while.*

43

Practice Book
© Harcourt • Grade 6

▶ **Which sentence makes more sense? Underline it.**

Word	Sentence 1	Sentence 2
1. intercept	Someone's got to *intercept* Mom or she'll never get up in time to write a note to my teacher.	Someone's got to *intercept* Mom and keep her from coming home before her surprise party.
2. seeped	Six inches of water in our living room indicated that water had *seeped* through the roof.	A stain on our living room ceiling indicated that water had *seeped* through the roof.
3. diagnosed	The doctors haven't *diagnosed* Jan's mystery illness.	The doctors know what Jan's illness is, but they haven't *diagnosed* it.
4. devoured	After the long hike, I *devoured* my dinner.	After snacking all day, I *devoured* my dinner.
5. lethal	A medicine should be *lethal* if taken as directed.	Some medicines may be *lethal* if not taken as directed.

▶ **Use what you know about the Vocabulary Words to answer the questions below. Write your answers in complete sentences.**

6. Why might someone make a *plea* while swimming?

_____

_____

7. What might you say to a friend if you are arranging a *rendezvous* at the movie theater?

_____

_____

School–Home Connection

With your child, discuss the Vocabulary Words. Have your child tell you what each one means. Ask him or her to use one of the words in a sentence about something that happened during the day.

44

Practice Book
© Harcourt • Grade 6

Name _____

▶ Read each section of "The Great Serum Race." Then complete the graphic organizers.

Section 1   pages 210–214

Detail	Detail	Detail

⬇   ⬇   ⬇

Main Idea
The residents of Nome needed antitoxin serum to cure a diphtheria outbreak. A dog team relay began to carry the serum to Nome.

Section 2   pages 215–221

Detail	Detail	Detail
People and dogs acted bravely in fierce winter conditions.	The serum arrived in Nome after six days on the trail.	The quarantine in Nome was lifted.

⬇   ⬇   ⬇

Main Idea

▶ Review your graphic organizers. Then, on a separate sheet of paper, write a summary of the selection.

► **Read the paragraph below. Then write your responses to the numbered items.**

Shortly after World War II, tensions arose between two of the world's most powerful countries. The United States and the Soviet Union had very different values. Neither wanted the other to be the world's only superpower. And both countries possessed many nuclear bombs. Just one of these terrible weapons could destroy an entire city. If a war broke out, experts warned, millions of innocent people would die. Children practiced air raid drills in school. Strangely, the fear of war prevented war from breaking out. For more than forty years, these two enemies built more and more weapons, but they fought only with words. This period is known as the Cold War.

1. What would be a good title for this paragraph?

   _____

2. In a sentence or two, briefly identify the main idea of this paragraph.

   _____

   _____

   _____

3. Write three important details from this paragraph that support the main idea.

   _____

   _____

   _____

4. Copy a sentence that you could delete from this paragraph without taking away from the main idea.

   _____

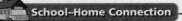
School–Home Connection

Ask whether your child had a good day or a bad day. Have him or her provide details that support the answer.

46

Name _____

▶ Fold the paper along the dotted line. As each Spelling Word is read aloud, write it in the blank. Then unfold your paper and check your work. Practice writing any Spelling Words you missed.

1. _____

2. _____

3. _____

4. _____

5. _____

6. _____

7. _____

8. _____

9. _____

10. _____

11. _____

12. _____

13. _____

14. _____

15. _____

16. _____

17. _____

18. _____

19. _____

20. _____

Spelling Words

1. report
2. climate
3. crusade
4. ego
5. retail
6. future
7. robot
8. humane
9. tiger
10. laser
11. lemon
12. limit
13. linen
14. major
15. minor
16. panel
17. sequel
18. valid
19. veto
20. vital

School–Home Connection

Have your child write the Spelling Words, underlining the words with a short vowel sound in the first syllable.

47

Practice Book
© Harcourt • Grade 6

▶ **Underline the independent clauses, and circle the dependent clauses.**

1. When we leave, you can drive, and we will sit in the back seat.

2. We want to see all the sights, if it is okay with you, and then we will head back.

3. Because Alaska is big, we cannot see everything, but let's see as much as possible.

4. The camera is out of film, but when we find a store, we can buy more.

5. Though we won't see all the sights, we will enjoy the trip, and we will take photos.

6. If we get lost, we can stop, and then we can ask for directions.

▶ **Combine each set of three sentences to write a compound-complex sentence.**

7. Temperatures are cold in Alaska. They get warmer in the summer. Many people enjoy Alaska during the summer.

   _____

   _____

8. It can be difficult to travel in Alaska during the winter. The terrain is icy. Many people visit during other seasons.

   _____

   _____

9. Many people enjoy living in Alaska. They like the breathtaking sights. They are willing to put up with the long winters.

   _____

   _____

10. Juneau is difficult to get to. It can only be reached by air or sea. There are no roads to or from the city.

    _____

    _____

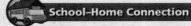

School–Home Connection

Ask your child to write two compound-complex sentences about a day at school. Then have your child point out the dependent and independent clauses in the sentences.

48

Name _____

▶ **Circle the letter of the best answer for each question.**

1. Which one is *equipped*?   **A** patient   **B** plumber   **C** customer

2. Which would be a good *reserve* to have in the desert?   **A** water   **B** flashlight   **C** parachute

3. On whom do you *rely*?   **A** enemy   **B** stranger   **C** friend

4. Which has a high *altitude*?   **A** plain   **B** valley   **C** mountain

5. To what *extent* does a goose giggle?   **A** always   **B** never   **C** sometimes

6. What would *hamper* you most?   **A** chains   **B** thread   **C** ribbon

7. Which news *overshadows* joy?   **A** good   **B** bad   **C** silly

▶ **Use what you know about the Vocabulary Words to answer the questions below. Write complete sentences.**

8. How would you get *equipped* for a bike ride? _____

_____

9. If your soccer team was *hampered* by too many absences, what would you do?

_____

_____

10. Describe the expression on your face when you have been *overshadowed* by

someone else. _____

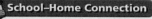
School–Home Connection

With your child, discuss the meaning of the
Vocabulary Words. Work together to use each
word in a sentence.

49

▶ Read each section of "Smokejumpers." Then complete the main idea and details charts.

Section 1 pages 234–237

Detail	Detail	Detail

↓ ↓ ↓

Main Idea
When a call comes to report a wildfire, smokejumpers quickly move into action.

Section 2 pages 238–242

Detail	Detail	Detail
They identify the safety zone.	They set up fire shelters.	They build a fireline and check for spot fires.

↓ ↓ ↓

Main Idea

Section 3 pages 243–245

Detail	Detail	Detail

↓ ↓ ↓

Main Idea

▶ Use the information in your charts to write a summary of the selection on a separate sheet of paper.

Read the paragraph. Then write your responses to the numbered items on the lines below.

In a large city, there are usually two types of firefighting companies: the engine companies and the ladder companies. Firefighters in each kind of company have difficult jobs. Both kinds of companies are equipped with specialized tools to fight fires. The engine companies respond to fire with hoses to put out the flames. Members of ladder companies are the ones who enter burning buildings to search for survivors. Most ladder companies assign firefighters to one of four different jobs, with specialized tools and equipment. The "can man" carries a fire-extinguisher canister which can be used to put out small fires during a search. The roof firefighter carries up to 130 pounds of gear, including a roof saw and 26 pounds of rope. The irons firefighter is equipped with an ax for breaking through doors and a special tool for forcing locks. The outside-ventilation firefighter pries or breaks open windows. All of the ladder firefighters carry a multipurpose entry tool called a Halligan.

1. What would be a good title for this paragraph? _____

2. What is the main idea of this paragraph?

_____

_____

3. Write three details you think are necessary to support the main idea of this

   paragraph. _____

   _____

   _____

4. What sentence could you delete from the paragraph because it doesn't support

   the main idea? _____

   _____

School–Home Connection

Work with your child to develop a statement about another type of worker who helps others, such as a police officer. Have your child think of three details to support the statement.

Practice Book
© Harcourt • Grade 6

Name _____

► **Read the paragraph. Then write each cause and effect in the chart.**

> Because of increased population, many urban centers in the United States are spreading out. As a result, more people are building homes in areas that border on wildlands. These places are called interface areas. Often homes in interface areas cannot be reached quickly by roads. When wildland fires occur, the buildings in interface areas are threatened. Families are in danger of losing their homes and possessions. Consequently, those homeowners must take precautions to protect their property.

1.

Cause	Effect
Population in urban areas increased.	

2.

Cause	Effect
Urban areas spread out.	

3.

Cause	Effect
	Families are in danger of losing their homes and possessions.

4.

Cause	Effect

School–Home Connection
Ask your child to identify the clue words that signal cause-and-effect relationships.

52

Name _____

▶ Fold the paper along the dotted line. As each Spelling
Word is read aloud, write it in the blank. Then unfold your
paper and check your work. Practice writing any Spelling
Words you missed.

1. _____

2. _____

3. _____

4. _____

5. _____

6. _____

7. _____

8. _____

9. _____

10. _____

11. _____

12. _____

13. _____

14. _____

15. _____

16. _____

17. _____

18. _____

19. _____

20. _____

Spelling Words

1. accept
2. adapt
3. adopt
4. affect
5. allusion
6. complement
7. compliment
8. device
9. devise
10. effect
11. except
12. formally
13. formerly
14. illusion
15. incite
16. insight
17. principal
18. principle
19. precede
20. proceed

School–Home Connection

Have your child write a story using at least ten
of the Spelling Words. Read the story together.
Check that your child used the words correctly.

53

Name _____

▶ **Rewrite each sentence. Replace the common noun in parentheses ( ) with a proper noun. Remember to use correct capitalization.**

1. (Name of city) is the capital of (state).

   _____

2. The (building) is in (city).

   _____

3. The (river) flows through (place).

   _____

4. (country) is part of (continent).

   _____

5. (relative) likes to go to (place).

   _____

▶ **Rewrite the sentences to correct mistakes in capitalization. Write the full words in place of the abbreviations in parentheses ( ).**

6. (Mr.) berkowitz is our science teacher.

   _____

7. Every (tues.), we do experiments.

   _____

8. During the experiments, we measure liquids in (ml) and we weigh powders in (g).

   _____

   _____

9. (prof.) jones was a guest teacher on (nov.) 18.

   _____

10. (Capt.) Small works at a Laboratory 10 (mi.) south of here.

   _____

Practice Book
© Harcourt • Grade 6

▶ **Read the Vocabulary Words. Then write the Vocabulary Word that best completes each sentence.**

alibi	concede	confidential	confront
culprit	justification	scandal	sheepishly
	unearthed	vying	

Most adults would **(1)** _____ that they need to take more time to relax. However, if you catch them just sitting, they often feel the need to offer some **(2)** _____. They seem to believe that others will **(3)** _____ them and charge them with "just loafing." How did we reach the point of feeling that too much vacation is a(n) **(4)** _____ and resting is a crime? You don't need a(n) **(5)** _____ when you take a day off!

Most people work hard at their jobs. **(6)** _____ for a promotion or just meeting the demands of the job can be stressful. In fact, medical science has **(7)** _____ some alarming facts about stress. It is the **(8)** _____ in many illnesses. Americans need to find ways to leave work behind more often.

▶ **Write the Vocabulary Word that best completes each sentence.**

9. A word that means the opposite of *boldly* is _____.

10. A word that means the opposite of *public* is _____.

11. A word that means the opposite of *dispute* is _____.

12. A word that means the opposite of *buried* is _____.

13. A word that means the opposite of *cooperating* is _____.

14. A word that means the opposite of *hero* is _____.

Practice Book
© Harcourt • Grade 6

▶ **Read the passage and then answer the questions.**

Jared called to his dog, "Farley! Here, Farley! Come here, boy!" But in answer, he heard only the measured chirping of crickets. It was ten at night and dark outside. Where could Farley be?

Jared had begged for months until, finally, his mom let him get the beagle. Jared thought he had never seen a cuter flop-eared dog. For the past two weeks, Jared and Farley had been inseparable. They played together and Jared even shared his lunch with Farley.

Three times a day, Jared was supposed to take Farley out for a walk. Tonight, it had gotten dark before Jared remembered, and Jared was terrified of the dark! He had thought, "Just this once, I will let Farley out by himself. He will surely come back!"

Now it had been half an hour and Farley was nowhere in sight. Jared felt terrible. Farley was lost, and it was his fault! He didn't have a choice—he had to go. He grabbed the leash and a flashlight, and stepped into the darkness.

He stumbled around the yard, calling his dog. Scary dark shapes loomed around him. Strange noises startled him. Still, he kept on. Finally, he heard a baying sound from the woods across the pasture behind the house. Farley! That was how he sounded when he chased a rabbit! Without thinking, Jared raced across the field. This time when he called, Farley heard him and came running with his tail wagging.

"Farley! You aren't supposed to run off like that!" Jared happily snapped the leash onto Farley's collar. As they started back to the house, Jared realized that his eyes had adjusted to the darkness. He could see just fine. Best of all, he wasn't a bit scared with Farley at his side.

1. Summarize the plot of the story.

   _____

   _____

2. What are three of Jared's character traits? What actions show these traits?

   _____

   _____

3. How do Jared's qualities affect the conflict and resolution of this story?

   _____

   _____

School–Home Connection

Ask your child to tell you the plot of a story he or she has read. Discuss what the main character's personality is like and how it affected story events.

56

▶ **Read the paragraph below. Then write your responses
to the numbered items on the lines provided.**

Meerkats, which live in colonies in the deserts of South Africa, teach their young about hunting using human-like techniques. A meerkat colony may contain as many as 40 meerkats. Many adults are "helpers" (not parents) who assist in raising the young. When the pups are about 30 days old, they begin to follow hunting parties of adults. The adult helpers make sure the young learn how to handle live prey. Over time, the pups are encouraged to approach live scorpions that have been disabled. Helpers may nudge the prey toward the young. These lessons are useful to the young meerkats. If the pups are not taught how to deal with dangerous live prey, they risk getting stung when they hunt for themselves.

1. What would be a good title for this paragraph?

   _____

2. Write one or two sentences briefly identifying the main idea of this paragraph.

   _____

   _____

3. Write several details necessary to support the main idea of this paragraph.

   _____

   _____

   _____

4. Write a sentence from the paragraph that does not support the main idea.

   _____

   _____

   _____

School–Home Connection

Work with your child to write a general,
true statement about a bird or other type of
animal. Have your child think of three or four
details to support the statement.

57

Name _____

▶ **Read each sentence and the words that follow it.
Then choose the word in parentheses that best
completes the sentence.**

1. The thief walked away _____ so the homeowners would not wake
   up. (quietly, calmly)

2. The next day, the whole neighborhood was abuzz with _____
   about the theft. (chat, gossip)

3. The homeowners said they had not seen anyone acting _____
   lately. (suspicious, jealous)

4. They were honestly _____ that anyone would take their hula-
   hoop collection. (amazed, startled)

5. Their daughter Amy, however, was _____ to lose her prize hula-
   hoop. (excited, devastated)

6. She believed it was taken by her _____ for the hula-hoop
   championship. (rival, enemy)

7. This person, however, had an _____ for the previous evening.
   (excuse, alibi)

▶ **Write sentences using three words that did not fit in the sentences above.
Make sure each sentence shows the word's precise meaning.**

_____

_____

_____

_____

_____

School–Home Connection

Ask your child to use the following pairs of
words in sentences that show how they are
different in meaning: *calm, sluggish; admiring,
flattering; gentle, soft.*

58

Practice Book
© Harcourt • Grade 6

► Read each sentence in column 1. In column 2, find the correct meaning of the italicized word as it is used in that sentence. Write the letter of the correct meaning on the line.

Sentence	Meaning
_____ 1. The hikers crossed a *stream*.	A. to gush or pour out freely
_____ 2. There was a steady *stream* of birds coming and going.	B. to move with a waving motion
_____ 3. Juice *streamed* from the pitcher.	C. a flowing body of water
_____ 4. The flag *streamed* in the wind.	D. continuous passage or flow
_____ 5. The mouth *parts* are needle-like.	E. to divide by combing in different directions
_____ 6. They divided the colony into *parts* for study.	F. portions of a whole
_____ 7. There are seven *parts* in the play.	G. roles for actors
_____ 8. She *parts* her hair on the right.	H. organs of a plant or animal

► Read the sentences. Circle the letter of the meaning that fits the context for the italicized word.

9. Once eggs *hatch*, the parent birds are busy getting food.

   A to produce young   C to think out or invent in secret

   B to mark with lines   D a small door or opening

10. The first *stage* of a bird's adult life is mating.

   A a raised platform   C a step in a process

   B a horse-drawn coach   D the plan of action for a notable event

School–Home Connection

With your child, brainstorm a list of different meanings for the word *foot*. Make up a sentence for each meaning.

Practice Book

▶ Fold the paper along the dotted line. As each Spelling
Word is read aloud, write it in the blank. Then unfold
your paper and check your work. Practice writing any
Spelling Words you missed.

1. _____

2. _____

3. _____

4. _____

5. _____

6. _____

7. _____

8. _____

9. _____

10. _____

11. _____

12. _____

13. _____

14. _____

15. _____

16. _____

17. _____

18. _____

19. _____

20. _____

Spelling Words

1. mangle
2. tickle
3. bridle
4. swindle
5. muzzle
6. bulletin
7. difficulty
8. exclude
9. survival
10. franchise
11. ego
12. linen
13. minor
14. veto
15. vital
16. complement
17. compliment
18. formally
19. formerly
20. precede

▶ Read this part of a student's rough draft. Then choose the best answer to each question that follows.

> (1) On Friday night the basketball team beat the Pirates and won the state championship. (2) During the game the crowd cheered wildly. (3) Although both teams were undefeated this season, the Bulldogs took the lead early _____ the game. (4) The league named Manuel Dias the Most Valuable Player _____ he kept the Bulldogs in the lead. (5) Dias almost did not play on Friday. (6) He recently hurt his knee.

1. Which preposition should be inserted in Sentence 3?
   A for
   B with
   C in
   D on

2. Which of the following is the prepositional phrase in Sentence 2?
   A During the game
   B the crowd cheered
   C the game the crowd
   D cheered wildly

3. Sentence 1 begins with which of the following?
   A a dependent clause
   B an independent clause
   C a phrase
   D a subordinating conjunction

4. Which two sentences can be combined with *because* to make a complex sentence?
   A Sentences 1 and 3
   B Sentences 2 and 3
   C Sentences 3 and 4
   D Sentences 5 and 6

5. Which is the subordinating conjunction in Sentence 3?
   A Although
   B both
   C early
   D in

6. Which subordinating conjunction should be inserted in Sentence 4?
   A when
   B because
   C although
   D which

▶ **Read this part of a student's rough draft. Then answer the questions that follow.**

> (1) Professor Brown will announce a plan to build a new Library. (2) The school will call the new library the "learning lab." (3) Since the Learning Lab will be twice as big as the Current library, it will have more books and periodicals. (4) The Learning Lab will have workspace for quiet group work. (5) Professor Brown will raise money, and he will ask the whole community for help, because the school board will not pay for the project.

1. Which of the following is incorrect in Sentence 1?
   A punctuation
   B no prepositional phrase
   C the capitalization of *Professor Brown*
   D the capitalization of *Library*

2. Which complex and simple sentences could be combined to make a compound-complex sentence?
   A Sentences 1 and 2
   B Sentences 2 and 4
   C Sentences 3 and 4
   D Sentences 1 and 4

3. Which type of sentence is Sentence 5?
   A simple
   B compound
   C compound-complex
   D complex

4. Which two words should be capitalized in Sentence 2?
   A new library
   B library, lab
   C learning, lab
   D school, library

5. Which abbreviation could be used in Sentences 1 and 5?
   A prof.
   B Prof.
   C Pr.
   D Mr.

6. Which word in Sentence 3 should be lowercase?
   A Learning
   B Lab
   C Since
   D Current

Name _____

▶ **Which example is better? Underline the sentence.**

Word	Example 1	Example 2
1. refuge	Sol goes to the mall to shop and hang out with friends.	Sol goes to her room to relax after a busy day.
2. phenomenon	The northern sky is full of dancing, multi-colored lights.	The sky is blue with scattered clouds.
3. bearable	Jaime put on cream to relieve her itching.	Jaime couldn't find anything to relieve her itching.
4. abundant	My uncle has fished here for years and has only caught an old boot.	My uncle says the fish here jump out of the lake and into his boat.

▶ **Use what you know about the Vocabulary Words to answer the questions below. Write your answers in complete sentences.**

5. Describe what someone who is *thriving* at school might be like.

_____

_____

6. What *illuminates* your classroom?

_____

_____

 School–Home Connection

Go over the Vocabulary Words with your child. Encourage him or her to think of another sentence that could serve as an example for each of the words.

63

▶ Before reading "Life Under Ice," fill in the first two columns
of the chart with what you know and what you want to know
about Antarctica. Then read each section and fill in the third
column with information you have learned.

K What I Know	W What I Want to Know	L What I Learned

▶ Review what you have learned from your chart. Then, on a separate sheet of paper,
write a summary of the selection.

▶ **Read the paragraph below. Then write your responses to the questions in complete sentences on the lines provided.**

(1) On the first night that we spent outdoors, angry waves lashed at the icy shore. (2) Clouds dashed across the sky, spitting ice and snow at the rocks below. (3) We huddled in our sleeping bags like frightened puppies. (4) Occasionally I could see the cold moon gazing down at us. (5) It was a distant lamp, offering no comfort to me or my companions. (6) The whole continent was like an enormous prison, I thought. (7) All night long, gloomy thoughts like these circled in my head like black-winged birds of prey. (8) When the sun finally smiled at us, I was able to smile back.

1. What kind of figurative language is found in sentence 1?

_____

2. What human qualities do the clouds have in sentence 2?

_____

3. Three sentences in this paragraph include similes. Which sentences are these?

_____

4. What human qualities does the moon have in sentence 4?

_____

5. Sentence 5 contains a metaphor. What is being compared?

_____

6. How do you know that sentence 8 includes an example of personification?

_____

School–Home Connection

Have your child read the paragraph aloud, stopping after each sentence to identify the examples of figurative language.

65

▶ Read the paragraph. Use the chart to help you determine the meaning of each underlined word. Then write the correct meaning on the line.

Prefix		Suffix		Root	
pre-	before	-able, -ible	able	dict	speak, say
in-	not	-ist	one who does	cred	belief
				port	carry

Because I scored high on my grammar <u>pretest</u> today, I was allowed to take one of the <u>portable</u> laptop computers to my desk and use the new art program. The graphics are <u>incredible</u>! In the advanced mode, <u>movable</u> puzzle pieces fall from the top of the screen and must be arranged into special color patterns to form digital pictures. I printed one of my masterpieces when I was finished, and my teacher said it looked like a real <u>artist</u> had made it. My father and older sister are lawyers, and most of my family likes to <u>predict</u> that I will be one, too. However, I would rather use graphics tablets than legal pads!

1. *Pretest* means _____.
   A a test given before material has been taught
   B a test that is not given

2. *Portable* means _____.
   A able to be carried
   B one who carries things

3. *Incredible* means _____.
   A not able to be believed
   B not able to be spoken

4. *Movable* means _____.
   A one who moves things
   B able to be moved

5. *Artist* means _____.
   A one who makes art
   B able to make art

6. *Predict* means _____.
   A said beforehand
   B not ever spoken

School–Home Connection
Ask your child to form other words by using the prefixes and suffixes in the chart.

Practice Book
© Harcourt • Grade 6

Name _____

▶ Fold the paper along the dotted line. As each Spelling
Word is read aloud, write it in the blank. Then unfold your
paper and check your work. Practice writing any Spelling
Words you missed.

1. _____

2. _____

3. _____

4. _____

5. _____

6. _____

7. _____

8. _____

9. _____

10. _____

11. _____

12. _____

13. _____

14. _____

15. _____

16. _____

17. _____

18. _____

19. _____

20. _____

Spelling Words

1. noticeable
2. passable
3. convertible
4. wearable
5. avoidable
6. predictable
7. profitable
8. applicable
9. accessible
10. breakable
11. destructible
12. excitable
13. recyclable
14. sensible
15. understandable
16. comprehensible
17. advisable
18. returnable
19. permissible
20. reproducible

School–Home Connection

Have your child write a story using at least ten
of the Spelling Words. Read the story together.

Practice Book
© Harcourt • Grade 6

Name _____

▶ **Write the correct plural form of each underlined noun.**

1. We watched <u>movie</u> about animals in a variety of climates.

   _____

2. The <u>penguin</u> waddled across the ice. _____

3. Some slipped and fell into snowy <u>ditch</u>. _____

4. Spotted <u>deer</u> raced through a forest. _____

5. Orange <u>butterfly</u> flew across the field. _____

6. Arctic <u>fox</u> have thick white fur. _____

7. Huge <u>moose</u> galloped into the distance. _____

8. Speckled <u>trout</u> swam in the stream. _____

▶ **Write the plural form of the noun. Then use the plural to write a sentence.**

9. camera _____

_____

10. hobby _____

_____

11. mouse _____

_____

12. bush _____

_____

School–Home Connection

Point to five items in your home. Ask your child
to write a singular noun to name each item.
Then have your child write the plural form of
each noun.

68

Practice Book

Name _____

▶ **Read the Vocabulary Words. Then write the Vocabulary**
Word that best completes each sentence.

> pelting   wedged   ideal   perched
> stranded   blurted   slunk

I thought it was an **(1)** _____ day for a bike ride until I hit a rock and

was **(2)** _____ in the middle of nowhere with a flat tire. While I was walking

my bike home, I saw a squirrel **(3)** _____ in a nearby tree. It was watching

as a cat slowly **(4)** _____ under the hedge. Suddenly the squirrel

(5) _____ out a loud screech. I looked and saw a baby squirrel

(6) _____ between the tree trunk and a rock. My initial reaction was

to begin **(7)** _____ the cat with some fruit snacks I had in my pocket.

I didn't want to hurt it—just scare it away.

▶ **Continue the story above. Choose three or more Vocabulary Words. Write a sentence**
for each word about what happened to the squirrels, the cat, and the narrator.

_____

_____

_____

_____

_____

_____

_____

_____

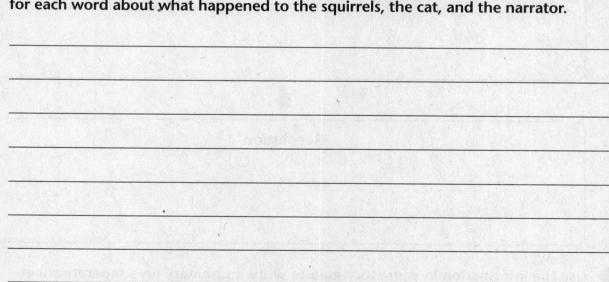

School–Home Connection

Your child is learning the above Vocabulary
Words this week. Have your child make
illustrations for at least three of the words.

▶ Fill in the story map as you read "The Long Bike Ride."

Characters	Setting

↓ ↓

Conflict

↓

Plot Events

↓

Resolution

▶ Use the information in your story map to write a summary on a separate sheet of paper.

Name _____

▶ Read each sentence. The word in parentheses tells the kind
of figurative language used in the sentence. Underline the
words that form the figurative language.

1. We swam like hungry sharks after a school of fish. (simile)

2. The calm sea told me to dip my toes into it. (personification)

3. The sea lion pup's eyes were like dark pools of ink. (simile)

4. At the edge of the beach the water was a lapping tongue. (metaphor)

5. The whale's fin looked like a drooping flag sticking up out of the water. (simile)

6. Tiny crabs scurried like ants running across the hot sand. (simile)

7. The turtle was as clumsy as a newly crawling baby as it came to shore. (simile)

8. The clouds were mounds of whipped cream moving across the sky. (metaphor)

▶ Write a sentence using each simile or metaphor.

9. as tall as a skyscraper _____

_____

10. was a bird in flight _____

_____

11. as loud as thunder _____

_____

12. is a fluffy chick _____

_____

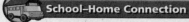

School–Home Connection

Your child identified and wrote sentences
containing figurative language. Work with
your child to identify examples of figurative
language in magazines or books.

71

Name _____

▶ **Fold the paper along the dotted line. As each Spelling
Word is read aloud, write it in the blank. Then unfold your
paper and check your work. Practice writing any Spelling
Words you missed.**

1. _____
2. _____
3. _____
4. _____
5. _____
6. _____
7. _____
8. _____
9. _____
10. _____
11. _____
12. _____
13. _____
14. _____
15. _____
16. _____
17. _____
18. _____
19. _____
20. _____

Spelling Words

1. poisonous
2. glamorous
3. joyous
4. adventurous
5. courageous
6. disastrous
7. luxurious
8. miraculous
9. studious
10. prosperous
11. envious
12. industrious
13. infectious
14. mysterious
15. suspicious
16. advantageous
17. spacious
18. nutritious
19. nauseous
20. outrageous

School–Home Connection

Have your child write two Spelling Words that
have a common letter so that they criss-cross.
Have them repeat until they write each word.

72

Name _____

▶ **Complete the phrase by writing the correct possessive noun.**

1. the swimsuit that belongs to a child: a _____ swimsuit

2. the beach ball that belongs to the girls: the _____ beach ball

3. the towels that a family owns: a _____ towels

4. the lunches that belong to the women: the _____ lunches

5. the basket that belongs to my grandparents: my _____ basket

6. the beaks of two birds: two _____ beaks

7. the fins of a fish: a _____ fins

8. the teeth of the whales: the _____ teeth

9. the pattern of the shell: the _____ pattern

▶ **Use the possessive form of the noun to write a sentence.**

10. mouse _____

_____

11. deer _____

_____

12. goose _____

_____

School–Home Connection

Ask your child to write the names of four
animals. Have your child write sentences that
include the singular and plural possessive
forms of each name.

73

Practice Book
© Harcourt • Grade 6

▶ Write the Vocabulary Word that goes with each idea.

| imperative | premonition | haphazardly | optimistic |
| disoriented | receded | remorse |

1. _____ sensing something

2. _____ looks on the bright side

3. _____ Right now!

4. _____ tide washing out

5. _____ to do something in a sloppy manner

6. _____ dazed and confused

7. _____ sorrow over an action

▶ Use what you know about the Vocabulary Words to answer the questions below.
Write complete sentences.

8. When might *remorse* be helpful?

_____

9. How can you tell if someone is an *optimistic* person?

_____

10. If you wrote a paper *haphazardly,* what might your teacher say?

_____

School–Home Connection

With your child, discuss the meaning of each
Vocabulary Word. Work together to write a
sentence for each word.

74

Name _____

Read each section of "Escaping the Giant Wave." Then fill in the corresponding section of your story map.

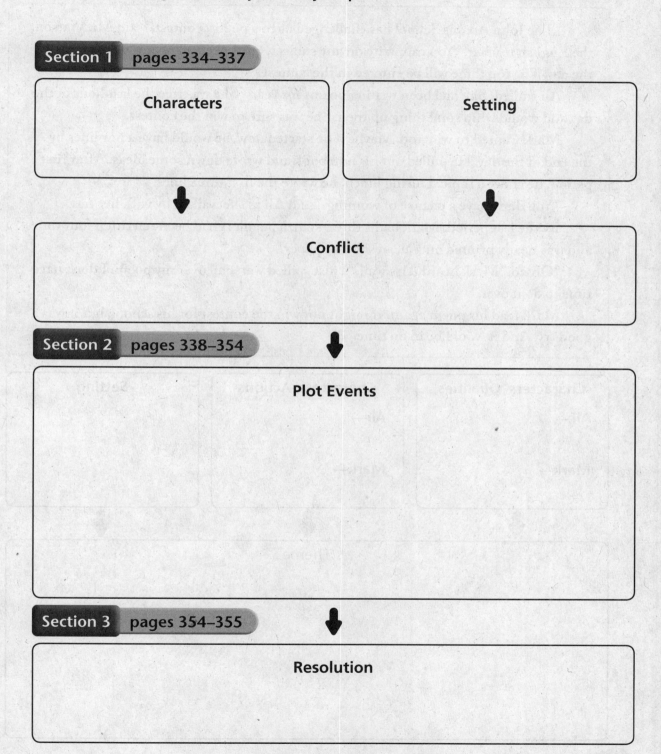

Section 1   pages 334–337

Characters	Setting

↓   ↓

Conflict

Section 2   pages 338–354

↓

Plot Events

Section 3   pages 354–355

↓

Resolution

▶ **Read the story below. Then fill in the graphic organizer.**

> "The John Adams School has challenged us to a poetry contest," said Mr. Watson, the English teacher. "You can write on any subject, but I need all poems by the end of the day. The top three will be entered in the contest."
>
> Ali smiled. She had been writing poems for years. She was free the last hour of the day and would whip something up then. She was sure to win the contest.
>
> Mark wanted to win, too. Maybe if he started now, he would have a few lines by the end of the day. He pulled out his notebook and wrote down some ideas. After first period, he chose a topic. During lunch, he wrote the first three lines.
>
> "You don't have a chance of winning," said Ali as she walked by with her tray.
>
> By the last period, Mark had a three-stanza poem. It had been rewritten four times and was neatly printed on a clean sheet of paper.
>
> "Oh no!" Mark heard Ali's wail. "I just spilled water all over my poem. I don't have time to do it over."
>
> Mark read his poem again. It might not win the contest for his school, but it was a good try. And it would be in on time.

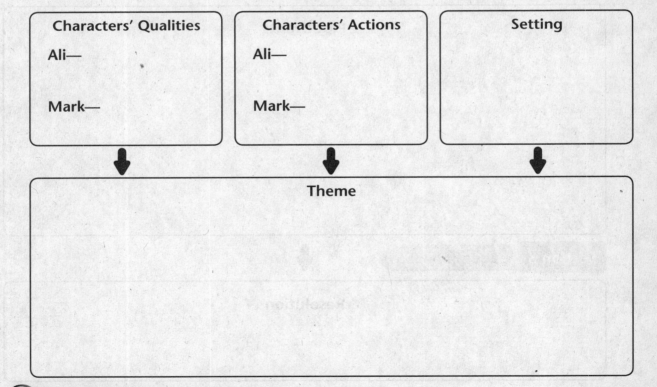

Characters' Qualities	Characters' Actions	Setting
Ali—	Ali—	
Mark—	Mark—	

Theme

School–Home Connection

Have your child reread a story he or she knows. Discuss qualities the characters have. Then have your child fill in a graphic organizer like the one on this page.

76

▶ **Each sentence below is a topic sentence for a story or an article. In the blank, write the author's purpose for writing. Choose from the following purposes: to entertain, to inform, or to persuade.**

1. Max was taking his dog for a walk when he saw something sparkle in the grass.

   _____

2. Once upon a time, in a kingdom far away, a lonely giant lived in the middle of a

   dark forest. _____

3. Dear Mom, I'm writing this letter to let you know why I would like to spend this

   summer on Grandpa's farm. _____

4. The Chinese invented many things we use today, including paper, boat rudders,

   fans, and spaghetti. _____

▶ **Write the first sentence for a story or article that fits each purpose listed below.**

to entertain: _____

_____

_____

to inform: _____

_____

_____

to persuade: _____

_____

_____

School–Home Connection

Work with your child to develop one of his or
her ideas into a story or an article. Make sure
all the details fit the purpose.

Name _____

► Fold the paper along the dotted line. As each Spelling
Word is read aloud, write it in the blank. Then unfold your
paper and check your work. Practice writing any Spelling
Words you missed.

1. _____

2. _____

3. _____

4. _____

5. _____

6. _____

7. _____

8. _____

9. _____

10. _____

11. _____

12. _____

13. _____

14. _____

15. _____

16. _____

17. _____

18. _____

19. _____

20. _____

Spelling Words

1. actual
2. beckon
3. burden
4. captain
5. comparison
6. example
7. foreign
8. people
9. informal
10. label
11. medal
12. peddle
13. personal
14. pigeon
15. several
16. special
17. sudden
18. natural
19. veteran
20. usual

School–Home Connection

Choose ten words and scramble the letters.
Have your child unscramble the letters and
write the Spelling Words.

Practice Book
© Harcourt • Grade 6

▶ **Write the correct pronoun to replace the underlined
word or words.**

1. Omar and his classmates arrived for a beach clean-up. _____

2. The teacher asked the students to work in pairs. _____

3. Ms. Kwan told the students to ask Mr. Johnson for trash bags. _____

4. Omar spied an old shoe, and he put the shoe in a trash bag. _____

5. Then Omar noticed unusual shells near Ms. Kwan. _____

6. Ms. Kwan was interested in discussing the shells with Omar. _____

▶ **Rewrite the sentences. Replace the incorrect pronouns with correct pronouns.**

7. Michael planted trees, so him could help Uncle Luke.

_____

8. "You and me will make a good team," Uncle Luke said.

_____

_____

9. Ann came by, and her helped with the planting.

_____

10. "Thanks for helping me and Michael," Uncle Luke said.

_____

_____

School–Home Connection

Have your child write four sentences, each of
which includes the name of one or more family
members. Then have your child rewrite the
sentences, replacing the nouns with pronouns.

▶ **Match the Vocabulary Word in the box with the situation it fits best. Write the word in the blank.**

| cocky | gingerly | terminal | rank |

1. Which word describes the way a person tries walking on a sprained ankle?

   _____

2. Which word best describes rotten food? _____

3. Which word describes a cold that never seems to go away? _____

4. Which word best describes someone with excessive pride? _____

▶ **Use what you know about the Vocabulary Words to answer the questions below. Write complete sentences.**

5. When was the last time you *winced*? What caused you to do this?

   _____

   _____

6. What is the difference between an *acquaintance* and a friend, in your opinion?

   _____

   _____

7. What possession would you be willing to *retrieve* from the trash if it were accidentally thrown away? Why?

   _____

   _____

8. What could you do when you are *stymied* about what to do for your mom on Mother's Day?

   _____

   _____

School–Home Connection

With your child, discuss the Vocabulary Words. Take turns using the words in sentences that tell about your day or a shared experience.

Practice Book
© Harcourt • Grade 6

Name _____

▶ Read each section of "Brian's Winter" and answer the
questions. Write your answers in the corresponding
sections of the story map.

Section 1 pages 368–373

• What are Brian's conflicts?
• What two plot events happen in this section?

Section 2 pages 374–376

• What routine develops between Brian and Betty? Add this to the plot events.

Section 3 pages 376–379

• What new plot event occurs? Add it to the story map.
• How is Brian's conflict resolved?

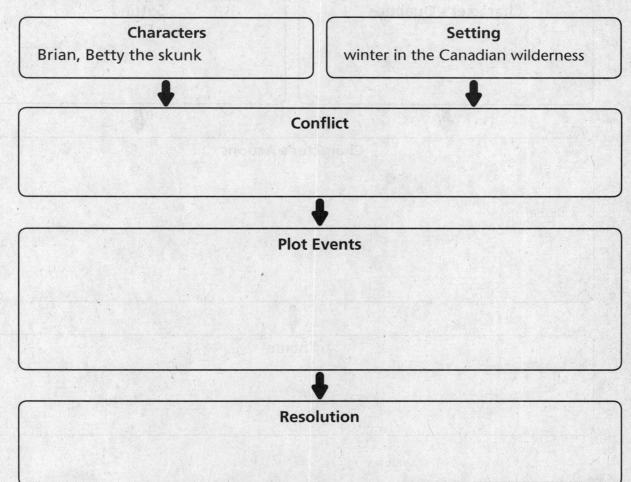

Characters
Brian, Betty the skunk

Setting
winter in the Canadian wilderness

Conflict

Plot Events

Resolution

Read the story below. Then fill in the graphic organizer with information from the text.

Penny didn't think she had a chance of earning the Outdoor Expert badge. She knew how to make a good fire and how to put it out safely. She also knew how to build a lean-to with branches. Those parts of the competition were timed, but she was confident she could finish within the time allowed. It was the five-mile hike that worried her. Contestants were given three hours and one canteen of water to make it up Bald Knob—a steep mountain with a rocky path. To prepare, Penny decided to exercise and strengthen her legs. Then she practiced walking up slopes. After a month, she felt much stronger. On the day of the event, Penny made it up the slope with ease. As she held her badge, she smiled happily.

Character's Qualities

Setting

Character's Actions

Theme

School–Home Connection
Read a short story with your child and work together to fill in a graphic organizer to identify the theme.

Name _____

▶ **Fold the paper along the dotted line. As each Spelling Word is read aloud, write it in the blank. Then unfold your paper and check your work. Practice writing any Spelling Words you missed.**

1. _____
2. _____
3. _____
4. _____
5. _____
6. _____
7. _____
8. _____
9. _____
10. _____
11. _____
12. _____
13. _____
14. _____
15. _____
16. _____
17. _____
18. _____
19. _____
20. _____

Spelling Words

1. beggar
2. burglar
3. cedar
4. computer
5. consumer
6. error
7. calendar
8. grammar
9. hanger
10. lumber
11. monitor
12. partner
13. pillar
14. prisoner
15. rumor
16. trader
17. traitor
18. vapor
19. vinegar
20. whimper

School–Home Connection

Read the Spelling Words aloud. Then have your child sort the words into two categories: words with two syllables and words with three syllables.

83

Name _____

▶ **Circle the appropriate possessive pronoun to complete each sentence.**

1. Next week, (theirs, our, mine, hers) school will celebrate Earth Day.

2. Has (yours, your, their, our) ever celebrated it?

3. Students at (mine, yours, ours, my) school have done research for months.

4. The students are ready to present (yours, mine, their, hers) projects.

5. Because Jan's presentation is more fragile than Bob's, she displays (its, hers, our, my) very carefully.

6. Unlike ours, Ana and Bob's project is about forests, and (your, theirs, its, her) may win a blue ribbon.

7. I hope people like the climate change display, because it's (my, our, mine, their).

8. Let me know whether (yours, theirs, mine, your) school ever celebrates Earth Day.

▶ **Underline the pronoun in each sentence. Then write *reflexive* or *indefinite* to describe the pronoun.**

9. Monday was a day when everyone wanted to sled. _____

10. None of the neighbors had expected so much snow. _____

11. Richard carried the sled to the hill himself. _____

12. The neighbors had been preparing themselves for sledding. _____

13. Richard heard someone yell, "Luz is going down the hill!" _____

14. Somebody was filming with a video camera. _____

15. Watching the video, Luz saw herself sledding. _____

School–Home Connection

Ask your child to write five phrases, each of which names an item and tells who owns that item. For each phrase, have him or her write a sentence with a possessive pronoun that refers to the item.

Practice Book
© Harcourt • Grade 6

Name _____

▶ Underline the sentence that uses the Vocabulary Word in a way that makes sense.

Sentence 1	Sentence 2
1. It is *prudent* to know when to go and when to stay.	It is *prudent* to never brush one's teeth.
2. Walking the sandy beach was *arduous* for us.	Walking the rocky trail was *arduous* for us.
3. Your impossible *demands* make it too hard to continue.	Your impossible *demands* made the meeting go smoothly.
4. I am *indebted* to you for the confusion at the train station.	I am *indebted* to you for your help at the train station.
5. The smile you showed me implied you were *dissatisfied* with the results.	The frown you showed me implied that you are *dissatisfied*.
6. Your phone call with the good news put me in a state of *bliss*.	Your disturbing phone call put me in a state of *bliss*.
7. I would rather have a *stationary* bridge than a swinging one.	I would rather have a *stationary* bridge than a solid one.
8. The letters on the top of the card were *entwined* to look like one.	The letters on the top of the card were *entwined* at opposite corners.
9. The *communal* bicycle race was for everyone in the neighborhood.	The *communal* bicycle race was by invitation only.
10. It became *apparent* that we knew the sun would shine next week.	It became *apparent* that the sun was going to shine.

School–Home Connection

Have your child read the sentences above. Then play a guessing game in which your child gives you a definition of one of the Vocabulary Words for you to guess.

85

Name _____

▶ **Read each sentence. Then identify the words that form
the type of figurative language listed in parentheses.**

1. Raphael tore through the crowd like a hurricane. (simile)

_____

2. Rain danced on the windowpane. (personification)

_____

3. The girl was a cat on tiptoe as she walked through the house. (metaphor)

_____

4. The flower grew toward the window for a kiss from the sun. (personification)

_____

5. The ball bounced as if it had a spring in it. (simile)

_____

▶ **Use each phrase below in a sentence of your own.**

6. as light as a balloon: _____

_____

7. laughing stars: _____

_____

8. like a tiger on the prowl: _____

_____

9. was a howling monkey: _____

_____

10. the pencil danced: _____

_____

School–Home Connection

Your child is reviewing figurative language.
With your child, read the sentences in the
second activity above. Then have him or her
tell you what kind of figurative language each
phrase is.

86

Practice Book
© Harcourt • Grade 6

▶ **Read each fable. Then write a theme that reflects its meaning.**

Cat and Mice

Some mice decided to hold a meeting about a certain cat that had been bothering them. They were trying to find a way to know of the cat's presence so that they might escape its clutches. One young mouse suggested a bell be tied around the cat's neck. It would ring whenever the cat was nearby, thus giving the mice a fighting chance. Everyone agreed that this was a good suggestion. A solution had been found. Then one older mouse cleared his throat and said, "I agree that a bell would solve our problem, but my question is, who among you is going to put the bell around the cat's neck?"

1. Theme: _____

2. What clues in the fable helped you to figure out its theme? _____

_____

_____

Crow's Plan

A very thirsty crow saw a pitcher with water in it. When he flew down to drink, he found that he could not get to the water. The mouth of the pitcher was narrow, and the water was too low to reach. The crow sat and thought. Then he saw some pebbles nearby and proceeded to drop them one by one into the pitcher. The water rose higher and higher until it was near the top of the pitcher, and the crow could finally get a drink to quench his thirst.

3. Theme: _____

4. What clues in the fable helped you to figure out its theme? _____

_____

_____

School–Home Connection

Your child is reviewing theme this week. Read the first fable above together. Then have your child explain the theme.

Practice Book
© Harcourt • Grade 6

Name _____

► Combine a prefix or suffix (or both) from Box A with a root
   or root word from Box B to complete each sentence.

Box A	Box B
prefixes: *in-, im-, re-, un-, de-* **suffixes:** *-ful, -ment, -ible*	**root words:** *able, assure, commit, correct, hope, take* **roots:** *cred, struct*

1. I was _____ to pass the test.

2. Most of their answers were _____, and they received a
   low grade.

3. I believed Lauren because her answers were _____.

4. The wrecking ball will _____ the buildings.

5. Jason will _____ the test next week.

6. Everyone should make a _____ to study.

7. Lauren was _____ that Jason could pass on his second try.

8. She tried to _____ him that he would do well.

► Make two more words using word parts from Box A, from Box B, or from other
   word parts you know. Use each word in a sentence of your own.

_____

_____

School–Home Connection

Your child is reviewing prefixes, suffixes, and
roots this week. Have your child read the
sentences he or she wrote above. Then help him
or her look in magazines and newspapers to
find other words that use prefixes or suffixes.

Practice Book
© Harcourt • Grade 6

Name _____

▶ Read the poem and look for the following poetic devices: repetition, rhyme, alliteration, onomatopoeia. Then answer the questions below.

Winter

(1) The ground was aglow—
(2) a reflection of stars on new snow below.
(3) The soft flutter of falling flakes
(4) had awakened birds from their sleep.
(5) They sang a distant chirp
(6) to a moon hung high over this clear, clear night.

1. What poetic device is used at the end of lines 1 and 2? _____

2. What words are used in line 3 to create alliteration? _____
_____

3. In what line did the poet use onomatopoeia? How do you know? _____
_____

4. What two poetic devices are used in line 6? _____

▶ Use poetic devices to write two lines from a poem. Identify the type of poetic device you use.

_____

_____

_____

_____

School–Home Connection

Your child is reviewing poetic devices. Read the poem above with your child. Have him or her explain the poetic devices used. Then work with your child to write a poem about another season.

89

Practice Book
© Harcourt • Grade 6

Fold the paper along the dotted line. As each Spelling Word is read aloud, write it in the blank. Then unfold your paper and check your work. Practice writing any Spelling Words you missed.

1. _____

2. _____

3. _____

4. _____

5. _____

6. _____

7. _____

8. _____

9. _____

10. _____

11. _____

12. _____

13. _____

14. _____

15. _____

16. _____

17. _____

18. _____

19. _____

20. _____

Spelling Words

1. convertible
2. breakable
3. sensible
4. permissible
5. profitable
6. glamorous
7. infectious
8. advantageous
9. gorgeous
10. joyous
11. beckon
12. example
13. foreign
14. informal
15. sudden
16. consumer
17. monitor
18. rumor
19. vinegar
20. whimper

Practice Book
© Harcourt • Grade 6

▶ **Read this part of a student's rough draft. Then answer the questions that follow.**

(1) The <u>butterfly</u> flitted among the bushes in the garden. (2) A monarch sipped nectar from the garden's many flowers. (3) Trouts glistened in the streams as the fish swam around the rocks and lily pads. (4) The peaceful scene was disturbed when a boy's bike slid into his friends' picnic table. (5) <u>Juan's</u> friends helped him get his bike out of the mud. (6) Then they pulled the <u>leaf</u> out of the spokes.

1. Which is the correct plural form of the underlined noun in Sentence 1?
   A butterfly
   B butterflys
   C butterflie
   D butterflies

2. Which change, if any, should be made to Sentence 2?
   A Change *garden's* to *gardens*.
   B Change *flowers* to *flowers'*.
   C Change *flowers* to *flower's*.
   D Make no change.

3. Which plural noun in Sentence 3 is NOT correct?
   A Trouts
   B streams
   C fish
   D pads

4. Which word in Sentence 4 is a singular possessive noun?
   A scene
   B boy's
   C bike
   D friends'

5. Which is the correct way to write the underlined noun in Sentence 5?
   A Juans
   B Juans'
   C Juane's
   D correct as is

6. Which is the correct plural form of the underlined noun in Sentence 6?
   A leaf's
   B leaves
   C leave's
   D leafs

▶ **Read this part of a student's rough draft. Then answer the questions that follow.**

> (1) Mia and Ralph wanted to build a birdhouse in their backyard, near the spot where they liked to have lunch. (2) They knew that everyone in town bought building supplies at Chang's Hardware. (3) Mia asked her dad for their help in bringing home the building supplies. (4) "Mom and I can both help you," Dad told her. (5) "Me and you together can get the supplies quickly," Mom said to Dad. (6) Within a few days, the family had built itself a new birdhouse.

1. Which word in Sentence 1 is a possessive pronoun?
   A Mia
   B Ralph
   C their
   D they

2. Which word in Sentence 2 is an indefinite pronoun?
   A They
   B everyone
   C Chang's
   D Hardware

3. Which pronoun should replace the underlined word in Sentence 3?
   A your
   B our
   C his
   D Make no change.

4. Which word in Sentence 4 is a subject pronoun?
   A Mom
   B I
   C you
   D her

5. Which change should be made to the underlined words in Sentence 5?
   A You and I
   B I and you
   C You and me
   D Make no change.

6. Which change should be made in Sentence 6?
   A Change *family* to *families*
   B Change *itself* to *themselves*.
   C Change *itself* to *it's*.
   D Make no change.

Name _____

▶ **Read the passage. Fill in each numbered blank with the Vocabulary Word from the box that best completes each sentence.**

meticulously	perfectionist	petition	counteracted
precise	regulates	trial	compensate

The problem with a (1) _____ is that he or she has to have everything right, down to the last detail. In writing, only the most (2) _____ word will do. In making something, every detail must be (3) _____ attended to. If a (4) _____ run for a project exposes a flaw, it's back to the drawing board. This need to do everything without mistakes ensures that the person (5) _____ all aspects of the project. Since I need someone with these qualities to run this experiment, I'm going to (6) _____ my instructor for a partner.

▶ **Write the Vocabulary Word that best completes each analogy.**

7. *Hot* is to *cold* as *sloppy* is to _____.

8. *Helpful* is to *beneficial* as *test* is to _____.

9. *Cheerful* is to *optimist* as *demanding* is to _____.

10. *Practices* is to *rehearses* as *controls* is to _____.

11. *Show* is to *demonstrate* as *make up for* is to _____.

12. *Destroyed* is to *damaged* as *prevented* is to _____.

School–Home Connection

Ask your child to make up an original sentence using each Vocabulary Word. The sentence should include a hint about the meaning of the Vocabulary Word.

Practice Book
© Harcourt • Grade 6

Name _____

► As you read "The Man Who Made Time Travel," fill in the sequence chart with events from John Harrison's life.

► Review the information in your graphic organizer. Then, on a separate sheet of paper, write a summary of the section.

Reader's Guide
Lesson 16

Practice Book
© Harcourt • Grade 6

Name _____

> Nevil Maskelyne sniffed impatiently as the clock was brought before the Board of Longitude. He was sure the monstrosity would not keep accurate time. After all, it had been cobbled together using cheap materials—mostly wood—and made by a mere carpenter! His own vast learning about the heavens told him certainly that the stars were a more reasonable and reliable resource for measuring longitude.

1. What is the point of view? _____

2. What clues tell you this? _____
_____
_____

3. This paragraph is an example of what genre? _____

> It was almost too much to bear! That self-important man carted away my precious clocks. The largest part of my life—all my years of thought and care and labor—rumbled away with them. I knew Maskelyne would leave no test untried and would subject them to every extreme of the elements in order to discredit my work. I could only turn my back. Then came the horrific, splintering noise. The careless laborers had dropped H1. It lay in fragments on the stones. At that moment, my heart seemed to shatter, too.

4. What is the point of view? _____

5. What clues tell you this? _____
_____
_____

6. This paragraph is an example of what genre? _____

95

Name _____

▶ Read about each foreign phrase. Then select a phrase from the box to complete each of the sentences in the paragraph below.

mea culpa	a Latin phrase meaning "I am to blame"
bon appetit	a French phrase that means "enjoy your food"
carte blanche	a French phrase that means that someone has unrestricted power to act on his or her own
bon voyage	a French expression meaning "have a good trip"
á la carte	a French phrase meaning "from the menu"

    As our friends wished us _____, we boarded the cruise ship. After we found our stateroom and unpacked our bags, we were ready for a bite to eat. To our surprise, everything in the dining room was _____. We had expected to have only buffet service. As soon as the waiter delivered our food and said "_____," the ship began to rock. We had hit some rough seas. When the waiter returned to refresh our drinks, the boat suddenly tilted. The drinks slid off his tray and onto our laps. The waiter was very apologetic and repeated one _____ after another. He later returned to our table with a complete set of clothes from the boutique on board. He also gave us _____ to help ourselves to anything in the dining room. Wow! We were definitely fans of this cruise line.

▶ Find another foreign word in the paragraph. Use a dictionary to describe what it means and to identify its origin.

_____

_____

_____

Practice Book
© Harcourt • Grade 6

Name _____

▶ Fold the paper along the dotted line. As each Spelling Word is read aloud, write it in the blank. Then unfold your paper and check your work. Practice writing any Spelling Words you missed.

1. _____
2. _____
3. _____
4. _____
5. _____
6. _____
7. _____
8. _____
9. _____
10. _____
11. _____
12. _____
13. _____
14. _____
15. _____
16. _____
17. _____
18. _____
19. _____
20. _____

Spelling Words

1. adobe
2. barbecue
3. barracuda
4. embargo
5. mosquito
6. patio
7. rodeo
8. sombrero
9. tornado
10. cargo
11. ballet
12. beret
13. bouquet
14. campaign
15. cassette
16. croissant
17. envelope
18. plateau
19. sergeant
20. depot

School–Home Connection

Have your child choose ten Spelling Words to illustrate. Ask him or her to label each picture with the Spelling Word it shows.

97

If the underlined adjective is correct, write *correct*. If not, write the correct adjective.

1. One of Gina's <u>least</u> favorite activities is making a schedule. _____

2. She likes to do <u>many</u> creative things than that. _____

3. Her <u>happier</u> moments of all are spent hammering and sawing. _____

4. Gina built the <u>longest</u> skate ramp in her neighborhood. _____

5. She also built the <u>large</u> of all the bookcases in her house. _____

6. Gina wanted <u>most</u> time to build than she already had. _____

7. She ended up spending <u>one</u> hour creating a schedule. _____

8. Following <u>that</u> schedule gave her more time to build. _____

9. Gina no longer thinks making a schedule is the <u>worse</u> thing to do. _____

Complete each sentence. Use the correct comparative form of the adjective in parentheses ( ).

10. John was flying on the _____ plane he had ever seen. (big)

11. From high in the sky, the cars looked _____ than ants. (small)

12. Frightened, John decided to be _____ about future travel. (careful)

13. He thought that the _____ way to travel might be by car. (good)

14. Then John saw one of the _____ sunsets ever. (beautiful)

15. Maybe flying was not the _____ way to travel, after all. (awful)

School–Home Connection

Name five things you see in your neighborhood. Ask your child to write them down. Challenge him or her to write as many adjectives as possible to describe each item.

98

▶ **Complete the sentence. Circle the letter of the ending that makes the most sense.**

1. A store owner might want to *publicize* an upcoming sale because _____.

   A advertisement attracts customers   C he's going on vacation

   B people love a good show   D his store is closed

2. Listening to music might be a *distraction* when you are _____.

   A dancing   C jogging in the park

   B at the beach   D doing your homework

3. A crowded restaurant is *testimony* to its _____.

   A good food   C bad service

   B menu colors   D high prices

4. When your clothes are *grimy,* you should _____.

   A wear them to bed   C bury them

   B wash them   D throw them away

5. The girl's *foresight* helped her to _____.

   A prevent rain from falling   C remember the past

   B avoid a problem   D see a movie next weekend

6. The *faint* sound we heard coming from outside was made by a _____.

   A lawnmower   C kitten

   B herd of elephants   D police siren

7. If a circus performer can do *contortions,* she can _____.

   A dance with trained tigers   C walk a tightrope

   B drive a clown car   D twist her body

School–Home Connection

With your child, discuss the Vocabulary Words and their meanings. Ask your child to read the sentences to you and explain why he or she chose each ending.

99

Name _____

▶ As you read "Maniac Magee," fill in the story map to help keep track of important events in the story.

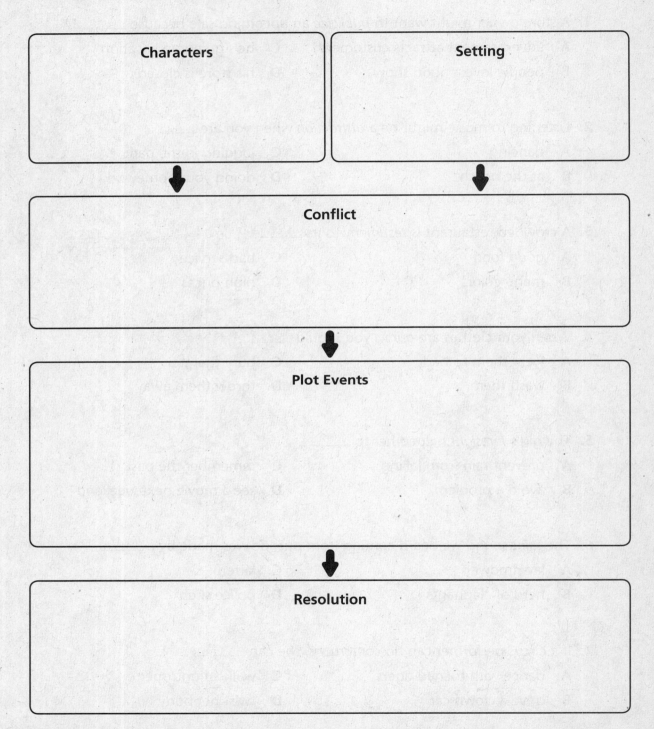

Characters

Setting

Conflict

Plot Events

Resolution

▶ Review the information in your story map. Then write a summary of the selection on a separate sheet of paper.

100

Practice Book
© Harcourt • Grade 6

Name _____

▶ **Read the story below. Then answer the questions in complete sentences.**

> ### The Inverted Hand-Walker
>
> Marshall Mathews could do one strange and amazing thing—he could walk for blocks on his hands. No one knew why or how he learned to do this. One day, it seemed, he just flipped his feet to the sky and began walking on the palms of his hands.
>
> "Well, he won't wear out his shoes," said his mother as she smiled nervously.
>
> "Yes," agreed his father, even though he felt the habit was rather bizarre.
>
> Mrs. Mathews sighed and shook her head. Long ago, she had stopped being concerned with what the neighbors thought of her unusual son. She knew that people would eventually realize that Marshall was very talented.

1. What is the point of view?

   _____

2. What clues tell you this?

   _____

   _____

   _____

3. Imagine that the story were told from first-person point of view. How would the story be different?

   _____

   _____

   _____

   _____

School–Home Connection

Read aloud a familiar story with your child, and have him or her identify from which point of view the story is written.

Practice Book
© Harcourt • Grade 6

Name _____

▶ Fold the paper along the dotted line. As each Spelling Word is read aloud, write it in the blank. Then unfold your paper and check your work. Practice writing any Spelling Words you missed.

1. _____

2. _____

3. _____

4. _____

5. _____

6. _____

7. _____

8. _____

9. _____

10. _____

11. _____

12. _____

13. _____

14. _____

15. _____

16. _____

17. _____

18. _____

19. _____

20. _____

Spelling Words

1. inability
2. inaccessible
3. inadequate
4. inadmissible
5. inappropriate
6. inattentive
7. impress
8. inaudible
9. indigestion
10. irrational
11. insecure
12. irresponsible
13. immobile
14. immovable
15. impartial
16. impassive
17. ineffective
18. illogical
19. illuminate
20. improper

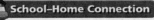 **School–Home Connection**

Have your child write the Spelling Words two times and cut the words apart. Turn the words face down and play a matching game together.

102

▶ **Circle each verb. Then identify it as** *main verb only* **or** *helping verb and main verb.*

1. Sports and art have both been important in our school.

   _____

2. We take them very seriously.

   _____

3. Each student has worked hard in an area of personal interest.

   _____

4. Did you see our case of trophies and awards?

   _____

▶ **Rewrite each sentence, adding a helping verb.**

5. Our team challenged another team to a volleyball competition.

   _____

6. The new student said he was a good volleyball player.

   _____

7. The net stretched across the field.

   _____

8. The players take their positions.

   _____

9. We played our best.

   _____

10. Our school achieved first place in the league.

   _____

School–Home Connection

Ask your child to look around outside your
home and tell you what is happening. Have
him or her write four sentences with helping
verbs to explain the action.

▶ Underline the sentence that uses the Vocabulary Word in a way that makes sense.

Sentence 1	Sentence 2
1. Everyone *marveled* when the cat licked her fur.	Everyone *marveled* when the cat found her way back home.
2. The *beacon* on the hill showed us the way to safety.	The *beacon* on the hill helped everyone hear better.
3. If we raise a *clamor*, maybe we can stop the barn from being torn down.	If we raise a *clamor*, maybe no one will pay attention to us.
4. The only *disturbance* was the fire sirens blaring all night long.	The only *disturbance* was the child's soft breathing.
5. She was so *enthralled* by the music that she started dancing in the store.	She was so *enthralled* by the music that she turned it off.
6. When the sore throat *persisted*, Sally's mother took her to the doctor.	When the sore throat *persisted*, Sally's mother was relieved.

▶ Use what you know about the Vocabulary Words to answer the questions below. Write complete sentences.

7. When might people have an *objection* to my playing the drums?

_____

_____

8. Why would it be a *coincidence* if two friends ran into each other in a distant city?

_____

_____

School–Home Connection

With your child, discuss the meaning of each Vocabulary Word. Ask your child to write a question using each word.

Practice Book
© Harcourt • Grade 6

Name _____

▶ Read each section of "The Kid Who Named Pluto." Then fill in the graphic organizers to identify the main idea and details for each section.

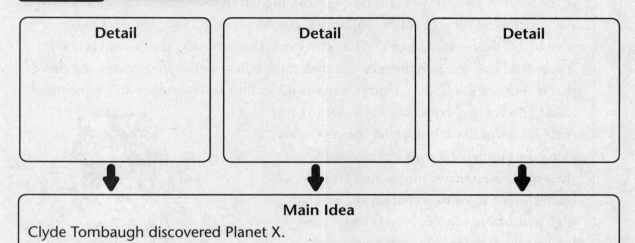

Section 1 pages 468–471

Detail	Detail	Detail

Main Idea
Clyde Tombaugh discovered Planet X.

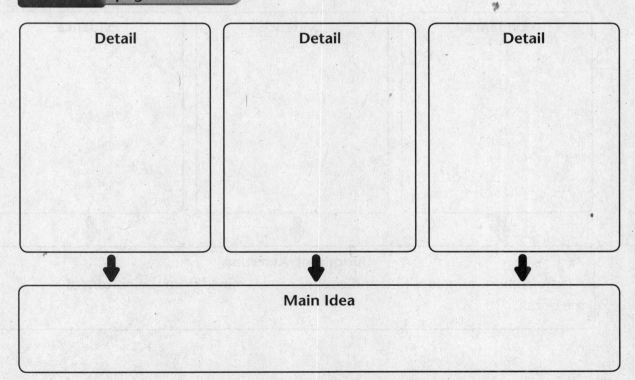

Section 2 pages 472–475

Detail	Detail	Detail

Main Idea

▶ Review your graphic organizer. Then write a summary of the selection.

Practice Book
© Harcourt • Grade 6

▶ **Read the paragraph. Then fill in the boxes with evidence from the paragraph that supports the judgment, or assertion.**

Scientists estimate that there are more than 25,000 underwater volcanoes, many of them active. When they erupt, hot gases stored deep inside earth rise up and dissolve the minerals on the sides of the volcanoes. The debris settles in a mound. One such mound, off the coast of Japan, is almost five miles underwater. The mound is really a "mountain" ten stories high and more than three miles in diameter. Scientists believe that it contains gold, silver, copper, and other precious and nonrenewable minerals and metals. So far, they have only been able to carry small lumps of the debris to the ocean's surface, using the mechanical arms on the outside of their small deep-water submarine. Tests done on the lumps show they contain an unusually high percentage of gold. Now scientists are looking for economical ways to extract the minerals and precious metals from the debris.

Evidence	**Evidence**	**Evidence**

Judgment/Assertion

A large amount of gold, silver, and copper can be mined from the bottom of the ocean.

School–Home Connection

With your child, try to think of evidence that would support the judgment that it is a waste of time searching for precious metals in the ocean floor.

Name _____

▶ Read the instructions on the application form for a library
card. Fill in the blanks with the proper information.

The Everytown Public Library
222 Main Street
Everytown, USA 00000

Library Card Application

Instructions: 1) Complete the application in full.
                  2) Sign the application.
                  3) Give the completed application to your teacher.

PART A   (Please Print)

LAST NAME _____ FIRST NAME _____

CITY _____ STATE _____ ZIP _____

E-MAIL ADDRESS _____

SCHOOL NAME _____

PART B
Please check the boxes next to the programs that most interest you:

☐ lectures   ☐ arts and crafts   ☐ homework help
☐ author readings   ☐ poetry contests   ☐ book fairs
☐ book clubs   ☐ workshops

Signature _____

Parent/Guardian Signature _____

STAFF USE ONLY: Date _____ ID NUMBER _____

School–Home Connection
Help your child get an application from your
local public library or another location and
work together to fill it out.

107

Name _____

▶ Fold the paper along the dotted line. As each Spelling Word is read aloud, write it in the blank. Then unfold your paper and check your work. Practice writing any Spelling Words you missed.

1. _____
2. _____
3. _____
4. _____
5. _____
6. _____
7. _____
8. _____
9. _____
10. _____
11. _____
12. _____
13. _____
14. _____
15. _____
16. _____
17. _____
18. _____
19. _____
20. _____

Spelling Words

1. compliant
2. contestant
3. immigrant
4. informant
5. inhabitant
6. significant
7. irritant
8. observant
9. resident
10. panelist
11. participant
12. scientist
13. biologist
14. columnist
15. medalist
16. cartoonist
17. pleasant
18. pollutant
19. obedient
20. confident

School–Home Connection

Write each of the Spelling Words backwards and have your child write the words correctly.

Practice Book
© Harcourt • Grade 6

Name _____

▶ **Identify the underlined word in each sentence as**
direct object **or** *indirect object.*

1. My neighbor gives <u>me</u> a book about the solar system. _____

2. I say that I will return <u>it</u> after I finish reading it. _____

3. I carefully read each <u>chapter</u> with great interest. _____

4. I return the book and tell my <u>friend</u> I really like it. _____

▶ **Write a sentence for each verb, using the form identified in parentheses ( ).**

5. feels (linking verb)

_____

6. feels (action verb)

_____

7. smells (linking)

_____

8. smells (action)

_____

9. looks (linking)

_____

10. looks (action)

_____

School–Home Connection
Ask your child to write four sentences about
a favorite family activity. Tell him or her to
use linking verbs in two of the sentences and
action verbs in the other two.

Practice Book
© Harcourt • Grade 6

▶ **Circle the letter of the best answer for each question.**

1. Which one is *eager*?

   A loser   B referee   C winner

2. What might be *neglected*?

   A chores   B parties   C movies

3. Which one is *severe*?

   A drizzle   B flurry   C downpour

4. Which one is *beloved*?

   A stranger   B friend   C enemy

5. Which one can be *demolished*?

   A river   B shopping center   C performance

6. Which might be *humongous*?

   A lake   B creek   C stream

7. Which might be *abandoned*?

   A ocean   B current   C ship

▶ **Use what you know about the Vocabulary Words to answer the questions below. Write complete sentences.**

8. Why might you be *eager* to do well on a test?

   _____

   _____

9. What would you wear in a *severe* snowstorm?

   _____

   _____

10. How would you feel if you had *demolished* your friend's science project?

   _____

   _____

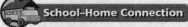

School–Home Connection

With your child, discuss the meaning of each
Vocabulary Word. Work together to use each
word in a sentence.

Practice Book

Name _____

▶ Read each section of "Buildings in Disguise." Then complete each chart below.

Section 1 pages 490–495

Detail	Detail	Detail

⬇ ⬇ ⬇

Main Idea
Lucy is an important example of mimetic architecture, and people want to preserve it.

Section 2 pages 496–499

Detail	Detail	Detail
The Big Duck was built to increase sales.	The Corn Palace showcased crops.	Larger Corn Palace buildings were built.

⬇ ⬇ ⬇

Main Idea

Section 3 pages 500–503

Detail	Detail	Detail

⬇ ⬇ ⬇

Main Idea

▶ Use the information in the charts to write a summary of the selection.

Practice Book
© Harcourt • Grade 6

Name _____

▶ **Read the paragraph below. Then write your responses to the numbered items on the lines provided.**

The Town Hall of River Village was 200 years old. It stood at the end of Main Street. Some historic town events had taken place there, but now, the building was in dreadful shape and was no longer being used. It needed a new heating system, and the roof needed to be replaced. The floors had rotted in many places and were unsafe. Wind, rain, and snow blew through the aging window frames. To repair and paint the exterior would cost many thousands of dollars. River Village had received a small-town grant from the state for the purpose of improving the quality of life in the town. The money could be used for new construction or for renovation. After much deliberation, the town leaders voted to use the funds to build a community swimming pool instead of restoring the Town Hall.

1. What assertion could you make about the Town Hall based on this paragraph?

   _____

   _____

2. Write three examples of evidence that you used to make your assertion.

   _____

   _____

   _____

3. Copy a sentence you could delete from the paragraph because it doesn't support your assertion.

   _____

4. What other evidence from the paragraph might support your assertion?

   _____

School–Home Connection

Work with your child to read a short newspaper article and make an assertion about it. Have your child point out evidence that supports the assertion.

Practice Book
© Harcourt • Grade 6

Fold the paper along the dotted line. As each Spelling Word is read aloud, write it in the blank. Then unfold your paper and check your work. Practice writing any Spelling Words you missed.

1. _____
2. _____
3. _____
4. _____
5. _____
6. _____
7. _____
8. _____
9. _____
10. _____
11. _____
12. _____
13. _____
14. _____
15. _____
16. _____
17. _____
18. _____
19. _____
20. _____

Spelling Words

1. overbearing
2. overcast
3. overconfident
4. overdevelop
5. overdraft
6. overhang
7. overindulge
8. overlay
9. overpower
10. undercarriage
11. underdone
12. underestimate
13. underrated
14. undertake
15. underwent
16. submerge
17. substandard
18. underground
19. subcontract
20. subtitle

School–Home Connection

Have your child write the prefix and base word for each Spelling Word on separate slips of paper. Use the slips to play a matching game.

113

Practice Book
© Harcourt • Grade 6

Name _____

▶ **If the underlined verb is correct, write** *correct*. **If not, write the verb correctly. Use the present tense.**

1. We <u>build</u> birdhouses for our science project. _____

2. They <u>is</u> part of the unit on animal habitats. _____

3. I <u>makes</u> the floor and walls. _____

4. My partner <u>hammer</u> the roof on top. _____

5. She <u>puts</u> the finished product into the car. _____

▶ **Write a sentence that begins with the pronoun given and includes the correct present-tense form of the verb in parentheses ( ).**

6. **I** (go)

_____

7. **He** (guess)

_____

8. **She** (design)

_____

9. **They** (have)

_____

10. **We** (take)

_____

11. **You** (run)

_____

12. **It** (be)

_____

School–Home Connection

Ask your child to write a short story that includes the correct forms of *sit, set, rise, raise, lie,* and *lay*. Invite him or her to share the story with you. Help your child check to see that present-tense subjects and verbs agree.

Practice Book
© Harcourt • Grade 6

▶ **Read the Vocabulary Words. Then write the Vocabulary Word that best completes each sentence.**

aficionados	astute	avid	brainchild
commemorate	conventional	traction	unison
	utilitarian	wage	

1. Was the big fundraiser your _____?

2. My parents consider themselves _____ when it comes to growing orchids.

3. The statute was erected to _____ their hard work and heroism.

4. Grandpa's old truck is strictly _____.

5. We are going to _____ a campaign to get a new playground.

6. _____ wisdom tells me that your plan will not succeed.

7. We sound like one voice when we sing in _____.

8. My brother is a(n) _____ golfer.

9. The girl made a(n) _____ observation about the magician's trick.

10. A car's rubber tires give it _____ on the road.

▶ **Write two new sentences using Vocabulary Words from the box above.**

11. _____

_____

12. _____

_____

School–Home Connection
Review the sentences your child wrote using the Vocabulary Words. Then have him or her define the Vocabulary Words listed in the box above.

▶ Read the passage below. It is told from third-person omniscient point of view. Rewrite the passage to show first-person point of view.

> Isabelle laced up her skates and took to the ice. She glided around twice before deciding to practice a few jumps and spins. She was glad to have the ice to herself this morning. It was hard getting practice in now that the ice rink was open to the public more often. She stopped and turned when she heard her name called. There were her friends, Colleen and Marla, who had their skates laced and were gliding toward her.
>
> "Trying to get a practice skate in?" Marla asked her. She smiled at Colleen, who winked at her. Both knew that Isabelle wanted to be a champion ice skater, and they loved to tease her about it.
>
> Isabelle shrugged and smiled. "Trying," she told them. "You know it'll be open to the public in half an hour, don't you?"
>
> "Of course," Colleen told her as she started to skate away. "That's why we came early, too!"

_____
_____
_____
_____
_____
_____
_____
_____
_____
_____
_____
_____

School–Home Connection

Your child is learning about point of view. Have your child read to you the passage he or she wrote and explain how it is the same as the one above it, told from a different point of view.

116

Name _____

Read the passage below. Then use complete sentences to answer the questions on the lines provided.

Lesson 20

Roald Engebreth Amundsen wanted to be the first person to reach the South Pole. He had dreamed of this adventure for a long time. Amundsen, a Norwegian, was descended from a long line of merchant sea captains and ship owners. He trained his body to adapt to the Polar Regions by sleeping at night with his windows open, even in winter. He led expeditions through the Northwest Passage between northern mainland Canada and its Arctic islands. This trip took three years to complete.

In the meantime, Ernest Shackleton, an Englishman, set out to be the first person to reach the South Pole. However, Shackleton's journey ended 97 miles short of his goal.

Amundsen's childhood dream was still alive. He studied Shackleton's mistakes to learn what to do and what not to do. Finally, Amundsen set out with his crew, which he had hand-picked for their seaworthiness and ability to handle the frigid Antarctic weather. Telling no one he was going south, Amundsen waited until the crew was well at sea before telling them his real destination. With stoutness of heart and a good plan, Amundsen and his crew reached the South Pole on December 14, 1911.

1. What assertions can you make about Amundsen?

_____

2. Cite two pieces of evidence for your assertion.

_____

_____

3. Why do you think Amundsen waited to tell his crew about the trip to the South Pole?

_____

_____

4. What assertions can you make about Shackleton?

_____

_____

School–Home Connection

This week your child is learning how to make judgments about a text. Review what your child has written above, and have him or her explain the answers given.

117

Practice Book
© Harcourt • Grade 6

Name _____

▶ Read the answers below. Notice that there are no questions
given. Choose a word from the box that matches each
answer and use it to write an appropriate question.

albatross	atlas	auburn	bagel
blank	cake	pajamas	taco

Question	Answer
1. _____	You wear these Persian-named clothes to bed.
2. _____	If you are lost, you might use a book of maps named for this Greek word.
3. _____	Someone's hair may be this French-named reddish-brown color.
4. _____	This Mexican word names a tortilla filled with chicken or beef.
5. _____	Sailors are wary of shooting down this Arabic-named bird.
6. _____	You might eat this Yiddish-named food for breakfast.
7. _____	This French word names an empty space to be filled in.
8. _____	We get the name of this sweet dessert from a Scandinavian word.

▶ Choose four words from above. Use the words to write two sentences about
something you like to do or eat. Use two words in each sentence.

_____

_____

_____

School–Home Connection

Your child is learning that some words in
English came from foreign languages. Have
your child read the sentences he or she created
and explain the meaning of the foreign words.

118

Name _____

▶ Read the instructions below. Then fill in the form.

VILLAGE OF ASHTON

Dog License Application

2007

Is the dog vaccinated? ____ No ____ Yes		For Village Use Only: License No. _____ Amount $_____ Date ___/___/__
Name	Last	First	Middle

Street Address	Telephone Number	

Dog's Name	Breed	Color	Gender

Vaccination Number	Date Vaccinated	Vaccinated By	

License Fee (any dog) $25.00	Change of Ownership Fee $5.00	Duplicate License Fee $1.00

Fee Enclosed	Signature of Owner	

LICENSE APPLICATION DUE MARCH 1	ALL DOGS OVER 2 MONTHS OF AGE MUST HAVE LICENSE	LICENSE EXPIRES IN FEBRUARY OF THE FOLLOWING YEAR

School–Home Connection

Your child reviewed how to fill in an application that asks for information. Discuss with your child the information he or she provided on the form.

119

Name _____

▶ Fold the paper along the dotted line. As each Spelling Word is read aloud, write it in the blank. Then unfold your paper and check your work. Practice writing any Spelling Words you missed.

1. _____

2. _____

3. _____

4. _____

5. _____

6. _____

7. _____

8. _____

9. _____

10. _____

11. _____

12. _____

13. _____

14. _____

15. _____

16. _____

17. _____

18. _____

19. _____

20. _____

Spelling Words

1. adobe
2. mosquito
3. tornado
4. bouquet
5. envelope
6. inability
7. irrational
8. immobile
9. illuminate
10. indigestion
11. informant
12. significant
13. participant
14. medalist
15. columnist
16. overdraft
17. overdevelop
18. underwent
19. submerge
20. subtitle

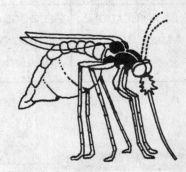

120

Name _____

▶ Read this part of a student's rough draft. Then answer the
questions that follow.

> (1) We had waited a week for our journalism teacher to post the newspaper
> staff assignments. (2) He had not want to give the assignments without serious
> planning. (3) He announced that he was posting the assignments when class
> ended. (4) He told us this year's decisions had been the more difficult ever.
> (5) The teacher held up the list and said, "This positions are for next semester."
> (6) He added, "I expect this to be the best staff we have ever had!"

1. Which words in Sentence 1 create a
   verb phrase?
   A had waited
   B waited a week
   C to post
   D staff assignments

2. Which is the correct way to write the
   underlined words in Sentence 2?
   A had not wants to give
   B do not wants to give
   C did not want to give
   D has not wants to gives

3. Which verb in Sentence 3 is a helping
   verb?
   A announced
   B was
   C posting
   D ended

4. Which is the correct way to write the
   underlined word in Sentence 4?
   A many
   B much
   C most
   D correct as is

5. Which is the correct way to write the
   underlined word in Sentence 5?
   A That
   B These
   C Them
   D correct as is

6. Which is the correct way to write the
   underlined word in Sentence 6?
   A better
   B most good
   C most best
   D correct as is

▶ **Read this part of a student's rough draft. Then answer the questions that follow.**

> (1) Celia watches as the plane rises high in the sky, and then she sets down on a bench to roll the newspapers. (2) She gives me a wave before she starts on her paper route through our neighborhood. (3) She carry the newspapers in a big bag over her shoulder. (4) Her paper route seems long today. (5) She feels happy when she finishes the route, but she looks exhausted. (6) Now, she have homework to finish!

1. Which change, if any, should the student make in Sentence 1?
   A Change *watches* to *watch*.
   B Change *rises* to *raises*.
   C Change *sets* to *sits*.
   D It is correct as it is.

2. Which word in Sentence 2 is an indirect object?
   A me
   B she
   C her
   D our

3. Which is the correct present-tense form of the underlined word in Sentence 3?
   A carrying
   B carries
   C carried
   D correct as is

4. Which identifies the underlined word in Sentence 4?
   A linking verb
   B predicate adjective
   C helping verb
   D predicate nominative

5. Which is true about the underlined verbs in Sentence 5?
   A Both are action verbs.
   B *Feels* is an action verb, and *looks* is a linking verb.
   C Both are linking verbs.
   D *Looks* is an action verb, and *feels* is a linking verb.

6. Which is the correct form of the underlined verb in Sentence 6?
   A is have
   B did having
   C has
   D correct as is

Name _____

▶ Read each Vocabulary Word and the two example sentences.
Then underline the sentence that gives the better example of
the Vocabulary Word's meaning.

Word	Sentence 1	Sentence 2
1. urges	This book is great! You must read it.	It doesn't really matter which book you read. They are all good.
2. influenced	Watching him hit the ball changed the way I play baseball.	No one taught me how to play. I learned on my own.
3. modern	We pump water by hand from a well at our summer cottage.	We have all the latest gadgets in our kitchen.
4. logic	Since we have been walking south all day, we must head north to return.	I have a hunch that the quickest way home will be in that direction.
5. promote	We have sold enough merchandise at the store without advertising.	We have put flyers about the sale under everyone's door.

▶ Use what you know about the Vocabulary Words to answer the questions below.
Write complete sentences.

6. Why should people in business have to study *ethics*?

_____

_____

7. What might someone in *pursuit* of popularity do?

_____

_____

8. Why might dogs be *banned* from a playground?

_____

_____

 **School–Home Connection**

Review the sentences above with your child.
Encourage him or her to think of another
sentence that could show the meaning of one
of the Vocabulary Words in items 1–5.

123

Name _____

▶ Read "Ancient Greece." Then write how you would complete the Venn diagram to compare and contrast the two people or events in each item.

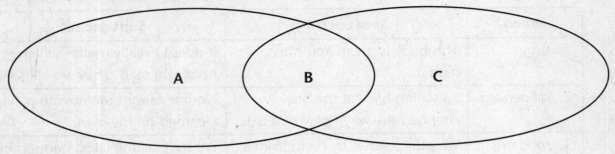

1. Herodotus and Aesop

   A. _____
   _____
   B. _____
   C. _____
   _____

2. Socrates and Plato

   A. _____
   _____
   B. _____
   C. _____
   _____

3. ancient Olympics and modern Olympics

   A. _____
   _____
   B. _____
   _____
   C. _____
   _____

Practice Book
© Harcourt • Grade 6

Name _____

▶ Read the paragraph below and fill in the Venn diagram. Put
information specific to Athens and Sparta in the appropriate
oval. Write information that is true about both cities in the
overlapping area.

Important Greek City-States

Athens and Sparta were both great city-states in ancient Greece. They were similar
in power and importance. Their governments, however, were very different. Athens was
a democracy, unlike Sparta, which was ruled by kings with absolute power. The citizens
of Athens were free to vote and express their opinions, but Spartans had few such rights.
Athens excelled in literature, architecture, and science. Sparta, on the other hand, was a
military state. Athens also had a powerful army and frequently went to war. When
a huge army from Persia attacked Greece, both Athens and Sparta fought against
the invader.

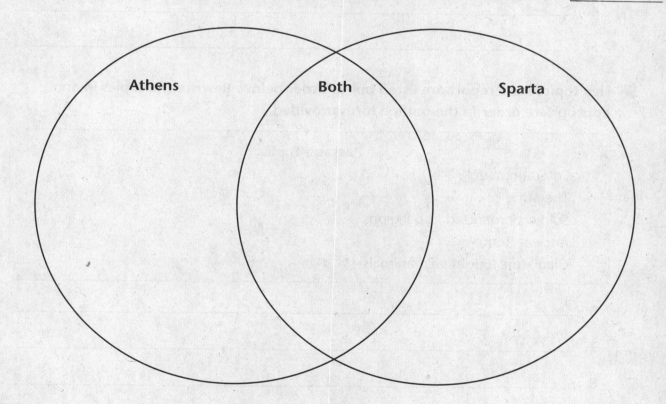

Athens   Both   Sparta

School–Home Connection

Ask your child to point out words and phrases
in the paragraph above that help explain the
similarities and differences.

Practice Book
© Harcourt • Grade 6

▶ The five steps of the SQ3R study technique are listed out of order below. Rewrite the steps in the correct order.

SQ3R Steps

Read the selection carefully.

Review your questions and answers.

Write questions to which you want to find the answers.

Survey the entire selection.

Recite the answers to your questions.

1. _____

2. _____

3. _____

4. _____

5. _____

▶ Five topics for a report are listed out of order below. Rewrite the topics in an appropriate order in the outline form provided.

Passage Topics

Entertainment

The army

Soldiers organized into legions

Ancient Rome

Gladiators fought wild animals

6. I. _____

7.   A. _____

8.   1. _____

9.   B. _____

10.   1. _____

School–Home Connection

Ask your child to choose any period in history that interests him or her and to show you how to make a K-W-L chart on the topic.

126

Name _____

▶ Fold the paper along the dotted line. As each Spelling Word is read aloud, write it in the blank. Then unfold your paper, and check your work. Practice spelling the words you missed.

1. _____
2. _____
3. _____
4. _____
5. _____
6. _____
7. _____
8. _____
9. _____
10. _____
11. _____
12. _____
13. _____
14. _____
15. _____
16. _____
17. _____
18. _____
19. _____
20. _____

Spelling Words

1. pedal
2. peddler
3. pedestrian
4. pedestal
5. dental
6. dentist
7. dentures
8. vocalize
9. manual
10. manuscript
11. manipulate
12. manufacture
13. vocalist
14. memoir
15. memorial
16. memorize
17. tripod
18. podium
19. memorable
20. maneuver

School–Home Connection

Hold a mini Spelling Bee. Call out the words and have your child spell them aloud. Ask him or her to write any misspelled words.

Practice Book
© Harcourt • Grade 6

▶ **If the underlined verb and its tense are correct in the
sentence, write *correct*. If they are not, write the correct
verb form.**

1. Tomorrow, we <u>worked</u> on our volleyball skills again. _____

2. We <u>play</u> to improve our volleyball skills last week. _____

3. Last Friday, the coach complimented the way we <u>will pass</u> the ball.

   _____

4. Yesterday afternoon, we <u>will practice</u> for two hours. _____

5. Last night, we <u>talked</u> about the new season. _____

6. At the meeting last night, the coach <u>hurry</u> to discuss everything.

   _____

7. Next year, we <u>competed</u> at a higher regional level. _____

▶ **Use the pronoun and the past-tense form of the verb to write a sentence.
Underline the correct past-tense form of the verb in your sentence.**

8. She; train

   _____

9. They; identify

   _____

10. We; jog

   _____

School–Home Connection

Ask your child to write sentences that include
the past tense and future tense of each of
these verbs: *cry, rake, rot, pop.*

128

Practice Book
© Harcourt • Grade 6

Name _____

► Read the passage. Fill in each blank with a Vocabulary
Word from the box. Use each word only once.

preceded	trespass	strategically	restored
prolong	resigned	temperaments	

The Tigris and Euphrates rivers flow from the mountains of modern-day Turkey

through Syria and Iraq, and on to the Persian Gulf. But what _____

these modern day countries? In ancient times the land between these two rivers was known

as Mesopotamia, a Greek word meaning "between two rivers."

Mesopotamia was a varied area with cedar trees in the northern mountains and wide,

barren plains in the south. In ancient times, people made the _____

sound decision to settle in this area to farm and enjoy the bounty that the land offered.

The climate suited their _____, and they soon established

cities. There were disputes, however, when people from neighboring cities would

_____ on each other's land. These disputes eventually were settled,

and one of the earliest civilizations, Sumer, was established here.

People in southern Mesopotamia were not at all _____ to

just living near the water; they thrived there. They learned how to irrigate their crops and

how to _____ the growing season using water from the rivers.

Mesopotamia was truly a lush and growing land.

Modern times have not been kind to this land, as wars and other disruptions have hurt

it. But slowly things are improving. Swampy areas that once were drained are now being

_____ to the glory that they once had. The rivers are being cleaned

up. Mesopotamia, the land between two rivers, will be beautiful once again.

► Write a sentence that explains what might make something *lustrous*.

_____

_____

_____

School–Home Connection

Your child is learning new Vocabulary Words
this week. Review the words with your child, and
have him or her tell you what each word means.

129

▶ As you read "The Emperor's Silent Army," look for the
items below that are compared or contrasted. Write the
similarities and differences in the Venn diagram.

"The Quest for Immortality" (pages 571–573)
Compare and contrast the emperor's tomb with his real world.

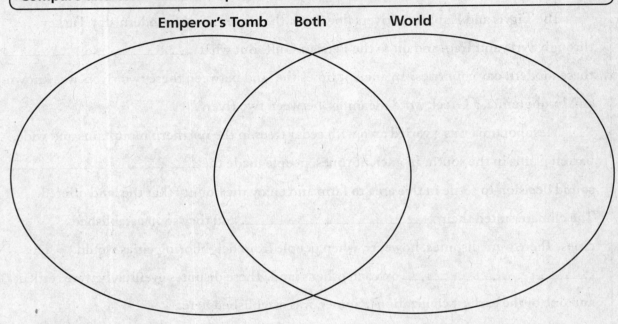

Emperor's Tomb   Both   World

"Buried Soldiers" (pages 573–576)
Compare and contrast Pit 1 with Pit 2.

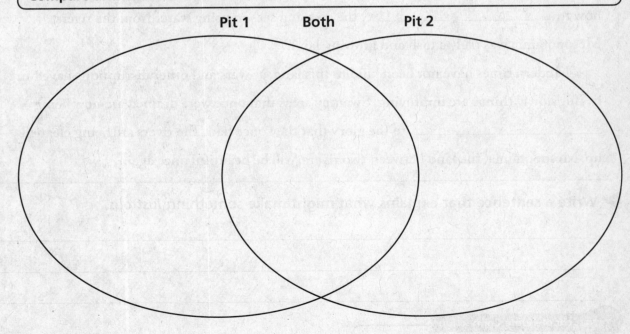

Pit 1   Both   Pit 2

Practice Book
© Harcourt • Grade 6

Name _____

► Read the passage below. Look for things that are compared
or contrasted, and write them in the chart.

The Incas of South America

The Incas had one of the largest civilizations of native peoples in the
Americas. But with an army of 40,000 soldiers, they were still no match for fewer
than 200 Spanish conquistadores. What happened to the Incan people in the 1500s?

A well-established society, the Incan empire consisted of various tribal groups.
When the Incan army captured a group of people, it assimilated those people into the
Incan empire. If the group pledged allegiance to the Incan ruler, its members were
treated as members of the empire. Although captured people were treated well, they were
not able to participate in the Incan political structure. Though they pledged loyalty to
the Incas, they were still considered a conquered people, and were subject to Incan rules.

The Spanish understood these policies and used them against the Incas. They
easily turned the conquered tribal groups against the Incan authority by making
promises to them. With a fighting force increased by the members of those tribes, the
Spanish used weapons that were far superior to Incan weaponry. With the death of the
central Incan authority, the Spanish managed to wipe out Incan rule and declare the
lands Spanish territory. By 1535, a great South American society had come to an abrupt
end. And Spain, not the Incas, ruled the New World empire.

Topic	Compare	Contrast
Spanish and Incan armies	Both the Spanish and the Incas had armies.	The Incas had 40,000 soldiers, while the Spanish had fewer than 200.
the Incas and the groups they conquered		
Spanish and Incan weapons		

School-Home Connection

Your child found comparisons and contrasts in
the passage above. With your child, look for
other comparisons and contrasts in magazines
or newspapers.

131

Name _____

► Use the information shown on the map of ancient
Greek city-states to answer the questions. Write
complete sentences.

Ancient Greek City-States

1. Which city-state is located the farthest south?

_____

2. What two seas are shown on the map?

_____

3. What is the name of the mountains in the west?

_____

4. Where is Mount Olympus located?

_____

5. What city-state is closest to Athens?

_____

School–Home Connection

Your child has been learning how to use
graphic aids to help in understanding
nonfiction texts. Help your child find and
interpret graphic aids in everyday reading,
including magazines and newspapers.

132

Name _____

▶ Fold the paper along the dotted line. As each Spelling Word is read aloud, write it in the blank. Then unfold your paper, and check your work. Practice spelling the words you missed.

1. _____
2. _____
3. _____
4. _____
5. _____
6. _____
7. _____
8. _____
9. _____
10. _____
11. _____
12. _____
13. _____
14. _____
15. _____
16. _____
17. _____
18. _____
19. _____
20. _____

Spelling Words

1. biology
2. biography
3. biome
4. democracy
5. epidemic
6. demonstrate
7. geology
8. geography
9. geometry
10. archaic
11. microwave
12. psychology
13. archaeology
14. microscopic
15. political
16. metropolis
17. police
18. cosmopolitan
19. policy
20. politician

School–Home Connection

Have your child sort the Spelling Words by their Greek and Latin word parts.

133

▶ **Circle the correct form of the verb in parentheses ( ).**

1. Athletes (had competed, are competing) in chariots long ago.

2. Chariots (are rolling, had rolled) around the track during the earliest Olympic Games.

3. Horses (had pulled, are pulling) them during those races many years ago.

4. Today, we (are watching, had watched) a film about chariot races.

5. Right now, the teacher (is looking, has looked) forward to teaching more information about chariots.

▶ **Write the present participle and the past participle of each verb. Then write a sentence that includes the specified verb part.**

6. fade _____

Sentence with present participle: _____

7. nod _____

Sentence with past participle: _____

8. find _____

Sentence with past participle: _____

9. display _____

Sentence with present participle: _____

10. hope _____

Sentence with present participle: _____

_____

School–Home Connection

Ask your child to write a sentence about a day at school. Have him or her use the present participle and the past participle of the verb *study*.

Name _____

▶ Underline the sentence that best uses the Vocabulary Word.

Sentence 1	Sentence 2
1. Everyone *tolerated* the loud noise from the street-cleaning machine.	Everyone *tolerated* the sunny day at the beach.
2. The group's *disposition* turned pleasant when they were refused entrance to the theater.	The group's *disposition* turned pleasant when the speaker finally arrived.
3. The *dispute* over what kinds of flowers to plant in the park became heated.	The *dispute* over what kinds of flowers to plant in the park made everyone happy.
4. It was *unsettling* knowing a tornado had been spotted.	It was *unsettling* to watch the sunrise.
5. She wore an apron *befitting* a princess.	She wore a gown *befitting* a princess.
6. The mother cat *vigilantly* watched over her newborn kittens.	The mother cat *vigilantly* watched over the pie baking in the oven.

▶ Use what you know about the Vocabulary Words to answer the questions below.
Write complete sentences.

7. When someone asks for a *savory* dish at a restaurant, what kind of food does he or she want to eat?

_____

_____

8. Why would someone be inspired by a *revered* person in the community?

_____

_____

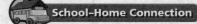

School–Home Connection

Ask your child to use the sentences above as examples for writing his or her own question and answer for each Vocabulary Word.

135

▶ Read "The Sons of the Dragon King." Complete character webs for the Dragon King and two of his sons. Write their traits in the outside ovals.

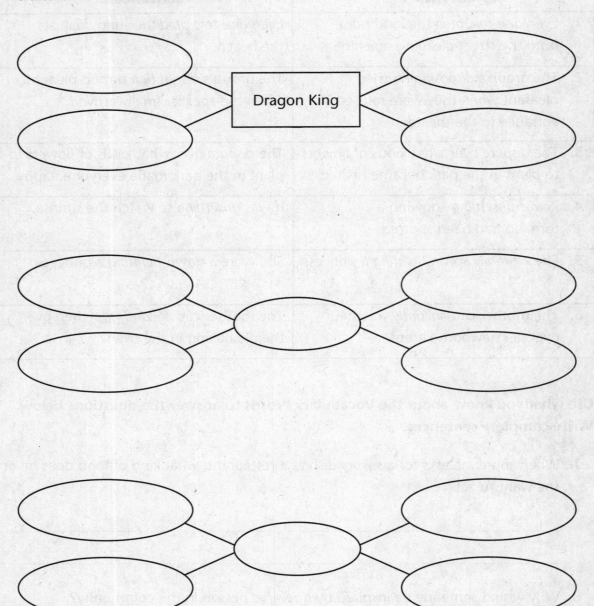

Dragon King

▶ Think about the information above and the other characters in "The Sons of the Dragon King." Then, on a separate sheet of paper, write a summary of the selection.

▶ **Read the paragraph. Then write an example from the paragraph for each literary device below. After the example, write a sentence about what the literary device stands for or shows.**

> Many years ago in a land of plenty, a young man set off to make his way in the world. He took with him his favorite horse. "Only when my steed and I prosper," he said, "will we return to our village." After many miles, they came to a valley with a stream. "We will work this land," said the man. But instead of going into the field, the man said, "My horse is so clever, he can plow the field by himself," and he took a nap. The horse worked the field until his back sagged and his hooves became sore from the rocks. He kept working until the crops grew tall, and then he hauled the grain away. He never complained, even though he became thin and weak while the young man became fat and his hands stayed soft. When the man and his horse returned to the village, the people saw the weak, thin horse and the fat man with soft hands, and they knew what had happened. They welcomed the horse with oats and with salve for its hooves. But the man they sent on his way.

1. Dialogue _____

_____

_____

2. Symbol _____

_____

_____

3. Mood and Tone _____

_____

_____

4. Irony _____

_____

_____

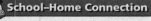
School–Home Connection
With your child, write a simple folktale using the literary devices of dialogue, symbol, irony, and mood and tone.

Practice Book
© Harcourt • Grade 6

Name _____

▶ **Fold the paper along the dotted line. As each Spelling Word is read aloud, write it in the blank. Then unfold your paper, and check your work. Practice spelling the words you missed.**

1. _____

2. _____

3. _____

4. _____

5. _____

6. _____

7. _____

8. _____

9. _____

10. _____

11. _____

12. _____

13. _____

14. _____

15. _____

16. _____

17. _____

18. _____

19. _____

20. _____

Spelling Words

1. polygon
2. monopoly
3. century
4. centimeter
5. quadruple
6. centennial
7. centipede
8. tricycle
9. triangle
10. diameter
11. dialogue
12. diagram
13. diagonal
14. biannual
15. bicoastal
16. bifocals
17. monochromatic
18. monarch
19. monologue
20. monotone

School–Home Connection

Assign each letter of the alphabet a number from 1 to 26. Then have your child write the Spelling Words along with their codes.

Practice Book

Name _____

▶ Circle the correct form of the verb. Then write the
infinitive form.

1. Only boys (go, went, gone) to school in the American colonies. _____

2. The students had (write, written, wrote) the alphabet many times.

   _____

3. If a student (speak, spoke, spoken) out of turn, he was punished. _____

4. They tried not to (come, came, comes) late to school. _____

▶ Write the stated form of each verb. Then write a sentence with that form.

5. draw   past tense: _____

   _____

6. draw   past participle: _____

   _____

7. drink   past tense: _____

   _____

8. drink   past participle: _____

   _____

9. eat   past tense: _____

   _____

10. eat   past participle: _____

   _____

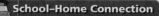

School–Home Connection

Ask your child to write four sentences about
history. In the four sentences, have your child
use the past tense and the present participle
of the verbs *to begin* and *to know*.

139

Name _____

▶ **Read each pair of sentences. Which sentence makes more sense? Underline it.**

Sentence 1	Sentence 2
1. *Primitive* people made tools from bones and rocks.	Cars are *primitive* compared to bikes.
2. The land by the river was *fertile*, and many crops grew there.	He was a fast kid and could run *fertile* and very far.
3. Sadly, the town was *flourishing* and many people were leaving.	The region was *flourishing* with new businesses and new people.
4. The Egyptians had special *rituals* for burying the dead.	The Egyptians liked to build *rituals* for their dead.
5. Without its nose, the Great Sphinx was *intact*.	The Great Sphinx is not *intact*, because it has no nose.
6. The walls were *reinforced* with heavy stones.	The walls were *reinforced* with many coats of paint.

▶ **Use what you know about the Vocabulary Words to answer the questions below. Write your answers in complete sentences.**

7. What would you want your *descendants* to know about you?

_____

_____

8. What are some ways that people are *immortalized*?

_____

_____

 School–Home Connection

With your child, discuss the Vocabulary Words.
Have your child tell you what each word means.
Ask him or her to think of two example
sentences.

Practice Book
© Harcourt • Grade 6

▶ Read "Secrets of the Sphinx." Use the K-W-L chart to help keep track of what you already know, what you want to know, and what you learned.

K	W	L
What I Know	**What I Want to Know**	**What I Learned**

▶ Review the information in your chart. On a separate sheet of paper, write a summary of the selection.

Name _____

▶ **Rewrite each sentence to make the imagery stronger. Make sure you use imagery that appeals to the sense that is shown in bold type.**

Example: The socks did not smell good.   **SMELL**

Answer: The socks smelled as if they had been left under a giant lump of rotting cheese.

1. The wool coat was uncomfortable.   **TOUCH**

_____

_____

2. The soup smelled good.   **SMELL**

_____

_____

3. The boy was crying.   **SIGHT**

_____

_____

4. The milk tasted awful.   **TASTE**

_____

_____

5. The sirens from the street were very loud.   **HEARING**

_____

_____

School–Home Connection

With your child, look through books or magazines to find sentences that appeal to the senses. Then discuss ways of changing the imagery or making it stronger.

Practice Book
© Harcourt • Grade 6

Name _____

▶ **Fold the paper along the dotted line. As each Spelling Word is read aloud, write it in the blank. Then unfold your paper, and check your work. Practice spelling the words you missed.**

1. _____

2. _____

3. _____

4. _____

5. _____

6. _____

7. _____

8. _____

9. _____

10. _____

11. _____

12. _____

13. _____

14. _____

15. _____

16. _____

17. _____

18. _____

19. _____

20. _____

Spelling Words

1. accusation
2. adaptation
3. animation
4. application
5. conversation
6. dehydration
7. destination
8. preparation
9. specialization
10. variation
11. definition
12. rejection
13. ignition
14. opposition
15. recognition
16. observation
17. emotion
18. duplication
19. celebration
20. transportation

School–Home Connection

Have your child write the Spelling Words. Then have him or her circle the word parts *-ation*, *-ition*, *-sion*, or *-ion* in each word.

143

Name _____

▶ **Circle the tense of the verb in each sentence.**

1. We will have gone on four field trips by the end of next semester.

    present perfect   past perfect   future perfect

2. We had visited the museum on one field trip last month.

    present perfect   past perfect   future perfect

3. Our class has looked for interesting places to go.

    present perfect   past perfect   future perfect

4. Earlier, the teacher had suggested a visit to the new exhibit on ancient Egypt.

    present perfect   past perfect   future perfect

▶ **Write a sentence using each verb in the tense shown in parentheses ( ).**

5. try (present perfect)

    _____

6. pay (future perfect)

    _____

7. think (past perfect)

    _____

8. give (past perfect)

    _____

9. provide (present perfect)

    _____

10. see (future perfect)

    _____

School–Home Connection

Ask your child to write three sentences about
a hobby. Have your child include one of the
following tenses in each sentence: present
perfect, past perfect, and future perfect.

Practice Book
© Harcourt • Grade 6

Name _____

▶ **Read the Vocabulary Words and the passage. Then fill in
the blanks in the passage with the Vocabulary Words that
best complete the sentences.**

overwhelming	ornery	aggravated	sophisticated
imposing	notable	prosperous	unassuming
	conspicuous	pillaged	

Kim loved her town. Because of its many successful businesses, it was

(1) _____. Its most (2) _____ feature

was an (3) _____ statue of one of the town's

(4)_____ mayors. Kim loved to sit in the courthouse park and

watch birds lounge on the statue.

But then a flood hit her town, and some people reacted badly. They

(5) _____ the businesses. They broke into the museum and stole

(6) _____ paintings off the walls. They even broke the statue of

the mayor.

Kim watched stories on the news and became (7) _____

about how her town was reacting. She had always been an (8) _____

person, but she became (9) _____ the more she learned.

"All of this is (10) _____," she thought. "I can sit

here being mad, or I can turn my anger into action." Kim put on her coat. She was

going to help clean up the damage.

▶ **On the blanks below, write a synonym, or a word that is close in meaning, for
each Vocabulary Word.**

11. overwhelming = _____

12. aggravated = _____

13. imposing = _____

14. ornery = _____

15. unassuming = _____

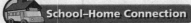

School–Home Connection
Have your child name an antonym for each
Vocabulary Word in items 11–15.

145

Name _____

▶ **Read the passage below. Then answer the questions in complete sentences.**

The graduation party was just around the corner, and Marcy and Jack had been chosen to decorate the gym for the festivities. The principal said they could decorate however they wanted, as long as they stayed within the budget.

Marcy had hardly slept the night before meeting with the principal. She was thinking of how the gym would look—pink and white streamers, floating balloons, and a big glittery sign.

Before he went to bed, Jack thought about plans for the decorations. He had drawn sketches and made lists. "We can make the gym look spooky," he told his mom, displaying his drawings. "The door will be draped with spider webs. We can keep the lights low. I can even play a recording of an owl hooting. Won't it be cool?"

Before school, Marcy and Jack met with the principal in the library. Marcy described her plans. She waved her hands to show streamers swaying back and forth. She released imaginary balloons. She described how the light would sparkle off the glittery sign.

When it was Jack's turn, he carefully clipped his drawings to the board. He pulled out his notebook and turned to the page marked *Proposal for Graduation Decorations*. In a firm voice, he read his lists. "I've priced all the items, and we are within budget," he announced.

1. How are Marcy and Jack similar in their thinking? _____

_____

2. How do they differ in their thinking? _____

_____

_____

3. How are Marcy and Jack different in their presentation styles? _____

_____

_____

School–Home Connection

Ask your child how he or she would decorate a space for a celebration. Compare and contrast your child's ideas with your own thoughts on decorating the same space.

Practice Book
© Harcourt • Grade 6

Name _____

▶ **Read the paragraph. Then fill in the chart with examples of the literary devices.**

Many years ago in an opening in a thick forest, there lived a father and his little son. They gathered juicy red berries for their breakfast, collected speckled eggs from their chickens for lunch, and had thick slabs of brown bread for dinner.

Yet, with all of this, the little boy couldn't help asking, "Papa, do you think there is another child for me to play with in this dark forest?"

The father said, "I will go into the forest and see if there is anyone for you to play with. Do not stray far from our house while I am gone."

"Yes, Papa," the boy said gleefully.

The boy waited by the window for his father to return. Then he went outside and sat under a tree. Soon he heard a rustle in the bushes.

It was a little chipmunk—and it could talk! "I am alone, too, and I'm looking for a friend. Would you like to play with me?"

When the father got home, he found the boy and the chipmunk snuggled together fast asleep by the warmth of the hearth.

Literary Device	Example
dialogue	
irony	
words for overall mood or tone	

School–Home Connection
Have your child locate and explain examples of imagery in the story.

Practice Book
© Harcourt • Grade 6

▶ **Each of the following situations describes a person's choice of a study technique. Tell whether the choice was good and why.**

1. Richard read a chapter about thermal energy. To help him study, he outlined the chapter after reading it.

   _____

   _____

   _____

   _____

2. Leanne made a K-W-L chart to help her study the ancient civilization in the Indus Valley. She had never heard of the Indus Valley before.

   _____

   _____

   _____

   _____

3. The next chapter in Kevin's social studies book is on economic policies in ancient China. Kevin wanted a complete guide to studying this chapter. He decided to use the SQ3R study technique.

   _____

   _____

   _____

   _____

School–Home Connection

Review with your child the study techniques described above. Have your child use one of the methods to study for a test or to prepare for an upcoming reading assignment.

Practice Book

▶ **Read the time line. Then write complete sentences to answer the questions.**

753 B.C. Rome founded;
753–509 B.C. Rule of
Etruscan Monarchy

264–146 B.C. Punic Wars

27 B.C. End of Republic,
Rise of Roman Empire;
27 B.C.– A.D. 14 Rule of
Augustus Caesar

509 B.C. Overthrow of
Monarchy, Beginning of
Roman Republic

60–49 B.C. Rule of Julius
Caesar

A.D. 476 End of
Roman Empire

1. What information is given in this time line?

   _____

   _____

2. What two rulers are noted on the time line?

   _____

   _____

3. In how many different forms did ancient Rome exist? What were they?

   _____

   _____

4. What wars are mentioned on the time line?

   _____

   _____

5. What do the numbers on the time line signify?

   _____

   _____

149

Name _____

▶ Fold the paper along the dotted line. As each Spelling Word
is read aloud, write it in the blank. Then unfold your paper
and check your work. Practice writing any Spelling Words
you missed.

1. _____

2. _____

3. _____

4. _____

5. _____

6. _____

7. _____

8. _____

9. _____

10. _____

11. _____

12. _____

13. _____

14. _____

15. _____

16. _____

17. _____

18. _____

19. _____

20. _____

Spelling Words

1. pedal
2. dentures
3. manuscript
4. memorial
5. tripod
6. memorable
7. biology
8. democracy
9. geography
10. archaeology
11. cosmopolitan
12. century
13. tricycle
14. diagram
15. bifocals
16. monotone
17. conversation
18. rejection
19. celebration
20. definition

Practice Book
© Harcourt • Grade 6

▶ **Read this part of a student's rough draft. Then answer the questions that follow.**

> (1) We <u>had worked</u> for hours last month to build a model sailboat for competition. (2) We learned of a problem with one of the sails when we first started. (3) We <u>will fix</u> it before we compete. (4) We are <u>thinking</u> about how to make the final adjustments. (5) Last week, the organizers of the competition _____ us all the information we needed. (6) Yesterday, we look at the plans to keep the model safe on the way to the competition.

1. Which form of the verb is underlined in Sentence 1?
   A past
   B past participle
   C present participle
   D infinitive

2. Which change, if any, should be made in Sentence 2?
   A Change *learned* to *learns*.
   B Change *learned* to *have learned*.
   C Change *learned* to *will have learned*.
   D Make no change.

3. Which is the tense of the underlined verb in Sentence 3?
   A future perfect tense
   B present tense
   C past tense
   D future tense

4. Which identifies the underlined verb form in Sentence 4?
   A present participle
   B past
   C past participle
   D infinitive

5. Which verb could complete Sentence 5?
   A have offered
   B has offered
   C will offer
   D offered

6. Which change, if any, should be made in Sentence 6?
   A Change *look* to *will look*.
   B Change *look* to *looked*.
   C Change *look* to *are looking*.
   D Make no change.

▶ **Read this part of a student's rough draft. Then answer the questions that follow.**

> (1) Today, my friend has taken a special trip to the lake. (2) When she comes back, she will have swum farther than any student in our school. (3) She has break every record in the county! (4) Last month, she _____ about ways to improve at her sport. (5) She _____ me a full report on the phone by the time she gets home. (6) I had make up my mind long ago to find a sport I enjoy as much as my friend enjoys swimming.

1. Which identifies the tense of the underlined verb in Sentence 1?
   A past
   B past perfect
   C infinitive
   D present perfect

2. How should the underlined verb in Sentence 2 be written?
   A had swum
   B had swimmed
   C will have swam
   D correct as is

3. Which change, if any, should be made in Sentence 3?
   A Change *has break* to *have breaked*.
   B Change *has break* to *has broken*.
   C Change *has break* to *broken*.
   D Make no change.

4. Which verb could complete Sentence 4?
   A had thought
   B is thinking
   C have thought
   D has thinked

5. Which verb could complete Sentence 5?
   A will has given
   B had gave
   C will have given
   D give

6. How should the underlined verb in Sentence 6 be written?
   A *have make*
   B *had made*
   C *am making*
   D correct as is

▶ **Read the Vocabulary Words in the box below. Then write the Vocabulary Word that best completes each sentence in the paragraph.**

impact	scale	barren	warped
mottled	distinctive	prominent	chasm

When viewed from Earth, the moon appears to have a face. This illusion comes from a (1) _____ pattern of dark and light regions on its surface. Up close, you see that the surface is (2) _____ by its many craters and irregularities. The craters formed long ago from the (3) _____ of asteroids striking the moon's surface. Covered with dust and rock, the uneven surface is (4) _____ of all life. Perhaps the most (5) _____ feature is the South Pole–Aitken Basin, a crater 1,550 miles in diameter.

▶ **Use a Vocabulary Word from the box above to complete each sentence.**

6. The opposite of *not easily seen* is _____.

7. The opposite of *fertile* is _____.

8. The opposite of *ordinary* is _____.

9. The opposite of *clear* is _____.

10. The opposite of *straight* is _____.

▶ **Write a sentence using the Vocabulary Word shown.**

11. scale _____

12. chasm _____

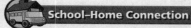
School–Home Connection

Ask your child to draw a picture or point out an object that illustrates the meaning of each Vocabulary Word.

153

Practice Book
© Harcourt • Grade 6

Name _____

▶ Before reading, fill in the first two columns of the K-W-L chart with information you know and want to know about our solar system. Then read "Next Stop Neptune: Experiencing the Solar System," and fill in the third column with information you learn from the selection.

K What I Know	W What I Want to Know	L What I Learned

▶ Use the information in your chart to help you write a summary of the selection on a separate sheet of paper.

▶ **Read the paragraph and the three numbered conclusions below. Write evidence from the paragraph that supports the conclusion.**

> If you live in the northern part of the Earth, you may get to see an amazing sight in the sky on clear nights. It's called the *aurora borealis*, which means "northern lights." The northern lights are great sheets of light in the sky that seem to wave and ripple. Watch closely and you may see flickers of red or green light, too. The sun causes the light show. The magnetic pole near the North Pole attracts particles from the sun. The northern lights occur when these particles collide with particles within the Earth's atmosphere and energy is given off. In the Southern Hemisphere, the same phenomenon occurs, but there it is called the *aurora australis*, or southern lights.

1. Without the sun, the *aurora borealis* would not exist.

_____

_____

_____

2. The *aurora australis* cannot be seen in cloudy weather.

_____

_____

_____

3. People who live near Earth's equator are unable to see the *aurora borealis*.

_____

_____

_____

_____

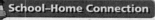

School–Home Connection

With your child, review the paragraph above and think of another conclusion you can draw from the evidence.

▶ Read the letter to the editor with numbered sentences below. Underline statements of opinion.

Dear Editor:

(1) This weekend we have an opportunity to experience something amazing. (2) Between midnight and 5 A.M. on Saturday, August 11, the Perseid meteor shower will occur. (3) The Perseid meteors become visible from Earth every year at about this time. (4) Because the skies will be clear Saturday night, conditions will be perfect for viewing the meteors.

(5) Meteors are rocks traveling through our solar system. (6) They are too small to be seen with the naked eye unless they enter our atmosphere. (7) If they do, friction makes them very hot, and we see the streak of light we call a "shooting star" or a "falling star." (8) Few things are as thrilling as seeing dozens of these graceful arcs of light streak across the night sky.

(9) Objects in the night sky are easier to see if you view them from a darkened location, away from city lights. (10) It means staying up late, but this show is so spectacular that we should all wake the family and have them watch it.

Sincerely,
Dr. Daniel Vesta
Professor of Astronomy

▶ Choose one of the facts from the letter above. Write the number of the sentence on the lines below. Then explain why it is a fact.

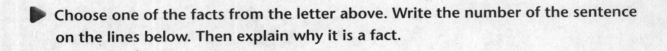

_____

_____

_____

_____

_____

School–Home Connection

With your child, brainstorm a list of opinions. For each opinion, state a fact that could be used to persuade someone to agree with the opinion.

156

Name _____

▶ Fold the paper along the dotted line. As each Spelling Word is read aloud, write it in the blank. Then unfold your paper and check your work. Practice writing any Spelling Words you missed.

1. _____
2. _____
3. _____
4. _____
5. _____
6. _____
7. _____
8. _____
9. _____
10. _____
11. _____
12. _____
13. _____
14. _____
15. _____
16. _____
17. _____
18. _____
19. _____
20. _____

Spelling Words

1. postponement
2. misinformation
3. uncertainly
4. improvement
5. indestructible
6. uncomfortable
7. unbeatable
8. unexpectedly
9. reexamination
10. unmistakable
11. telescope
12. thermometer
13. microscope
14. mischievous
15. prescription
16. telephone
17. octopus
18. process
19. transport
20. aquatic

School–Home Connection

Have your child write the Spelling Words in alphabetical order and then in reverse alphabetical order.

Practice Book
© Harcourt • Grade 6

▶ Circle the progressive-verb phrase. If it is correct, write
correct. If it is not, write the correct progressive-verb phrase.

1. Last month, we will be doing experiments. _____

2. During the past week, we are starting new experiments. _____

3. I was writing experiment results last week. _____

4. The teacher will be giving new information yesterday. _____

5. We will be finishing the experiments next week. _____

6. Next year, students were completing new experiments. _____

▶ Replace each past-tense verb with its past-progressive form, each present-tense
verb with its present-progressive form, and each future-tense verb with its
future-progressive form.

7. The sunspots (interfered) _____ with radio reception.

8. Scientists (predicted) _____ ongoing problems.

9. They (do) _____ all they can to learn more about sunspots.

10. Next year, the sunspots (will occur) _____ often.

11. Researchers (write) _____ about the effects of sunspots.

12. One day, researchers (will discover) _____
even more.

13. I (hope) _____ to study astronomy in college.

14. I (looked) _____ into the best programs last year.

15. My aunt and I (drove) _____ to visit a nearby college.

Practice Book
© Harcourt • Grade 6

Name _____

▶ Read the Vocabulary Words in the box below. Then write
the Vocabulary Word that best completes each sentence
in the paragraph.

murky	remains	lavish
doomed	dreaded	ascent

Our annual Fourth of July party was a gala event. The picnic table groaned under

the weight of a (1) _____ spread of food. Earlier in the week, we had feared

the party would be (2) _____ because of thunderstorms, but the day dawned

brilliant and clear. Once everyone had feasted, we whisked the (3) _____ of

our feast into the refrigerator. By then it was dusk and the evening sky had grown

(4) _____. But our moods weren't dampened, because it was time for

fireworks! In the darkness, we traced the (5) _____ of the flares and waited

for the glorious explosions of color, shape, and light. Only the dog trembled and hid

from the (6) _____ noise.

▶ Write the Vocabulary Word that best completes each sentence.

7. A word that means the same as *fancy* is _____.

8. A word that means the same as *leftovers* is _____.

9. A word that means the same as *climb* is _____.

10. A word that means the same as *feared* is _____.

11. A word that means *sure to be ruined* is _____.

12. A word that means the same as *dark* is _____.

School–Home Connection

Have your child write each Vocabulary Word
on a card. Every day, "feature" a new word at
mealtimes. See who can use the word the most
times in conversation.

159

Practice Book
© Harcourt • Grade 6

▶ Read each section of "The Incredible Quest to Find the *Titanic*." Then fill in the chart with the main idea and the supporting details of the section.

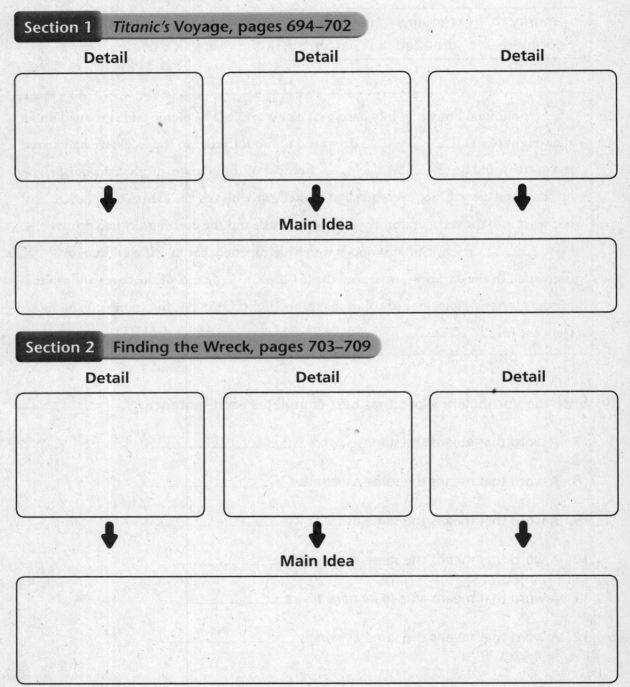

Section 1 *Titanic's* Voyage, pages 694–702

Detail

Detail

Detail

Main Idea

Section 2 Finding the Wreck, pages 703–709

Detail

Detail

Detail

Main Idea

▶ Use the information in your charts to write a summary of the selection on a separate sheet of paper.

Practice Book
© Harcourt • Grade 6

▶ Read the paragraph below and underline the author's conclusion. On the lines, write evidence that supports the conclusion.

> At 2:20 A.M. on April 15, 1912, *Titanic* sank to the ocean floor. To reach it, explorers had to descend 12,400 feet, or more than 2 miles. To understand what this was like, consider these facts. No scuba diver has gone more than 437 feet beneath the surface. Naval submarines will only go down 1,500 feet. Beyond this, the ocean is in total blackness. In waters a mile deep, one might see glowing sea creatures. At two miles, there is only darkness, crushing pressure, and water just above the freezing point. To reach *Titanic*, explorers risked great danger.

_____

_____

_____

▶ Read the paragraph below and use the evidence given to draw a conclusion. Then write an explanation of why your conclusion is valid.

> Of the 2,228 people on board *Titanic*, just over 700 survived. That is less than 32 percent. However, if you look at the survivors based on their wealth, the numbers are different. Sixty percent of all first-class passengers lived; this number included most of the women and children in first class. Forty-four percent of second-class passengers made it to lifeboats. But of the poorest passengers, only 25 percent survived. Fewer than half of the women and children in steerage lived to tell their stories.

Conclusion:

_____

_____

Explanation:

_____

_____

School–Home Connection

With your child, reread the first paragraph above. Think of another conclusion that could be drawn from the facts.

161

Name _____

▶ For each word in bold type in the first column, write a
synonym that you associate with favorable or positive
feelings and another synonym that causes unfavorable or
negative feelings. Use a dictionary or thesaurus if you need help.

Neutral Word	Synonym with Positive Connotation	Synonym with Negative Connotation
1. a **large** helping		
2. **old** furniture		
3. **ask** for help		
4. **talk** about an issue		
5. make a **joke**		
6. a noticeable **aroma**		

▶ Write four sentences, using a synonym from the table in each to create a positive
or negative connotation.

7. _____

_____

8. _____

_____

9. _____

_____

10. _____

_____

School–Home Connection

With your child, read a letter to the editor.
Highlight words that have strong negative or
positive connotations, and discuss their effect.

162

▶ **Fold the paper along the dotted line. As each Spelling Word is read aloud, write it in the blank. Then unfold your paper and check your work. Practice writing any Spelling Words you missed.**

1. _____

2. _____

3. _____

4. _____

5. _____

6. _____

7. _____

8. _____

9. _____

10. _____

11. _____

12. _____

13. _____

14. _____

15. _____

16. _____

17. _____

18. _____

19. _____

20. _____

Spelling Words

1. aisle
2. align
3. rhythm
4. crumbs
5. fasten
6. glistened
7. knotty
8. knuckle
9. often
10. plumber
11. reign
12. bustle
13. shepherd
14. soften
15. sword
16. thistle
17. knock
18. wrestle
19. wrinkled
20. yolk

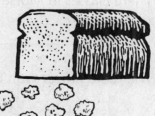

School–Home Connection

Have your child write the Spelling Words and
draw a line through the silent letter or letters.

163

Name _____

▶ **Write a contraction to correctly complete each sentence.**

1. We knew that _____ better hurry if we wanted to be on time.

2. "What will happen if we do not get to the dock before _____ time to sail?" I asked.

3. "_____ going to be on time," my grandmother said.

4. _____ waving to us from the house.

5. If we call ahead, I think _____ wait for us.

6. _____ right; that is a very good idea.

▶ **If the sentence is correct, write *correct*. If it is not, write the sentence correctly.**

7. The Morse code book is your's.

_____

8. I saw the old Morse code book, and it's cover was torn.

_____

9. The radio officer said we were the best students of all.

_____

10. I can'not read the author's name on the cover.

_____

11. There classes in Morse code are excellent.

_____

12. The radio officer won't be late to class today.

_____

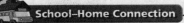
School–Home Connection

Ask your child to write the contractions for:
there is; we are; will not; cannot. Then have
your child use each contraction in a sentence.

Practice Book
© Harcourt • Grade 6

▶ Underline the sentence that best uses the Vocabulary Word.

Sentence 1	Sentence 2
1. Simon looked *contentedly* at the lettuce plants the rabbit had eaten.	Simon looked *contentedly* at the thriving lettuce plants in his garden.
2. Sid had *qualms* about riding the tandem bicycle for the first time.	Sid had *qualms* about riding the tandem bicycle with an instructor.
3. The *torrent* of water made everything that was in the park sticky.	The *torrent* of water washed away the layer of mud on the picnic table.
4. You can *endanger* a butterfly by putting it inside a jar.	You can *endanger* a butterfly by watching it fly outdoors.
5. *Contemplating* a project before I start helps me do it right.	*Contemplating* a project before I start is a waste of time.
6. The bicycle path was *intolerable* because it was smooth and flat.	The bicycle path was *intolerable* because it was filled with rocks.

▶ Use what you know about the Vocabulary Words to answer the questions below. Write complete sentences.

7. How might an *officious* person act while waiting in line for something?

_____

_____

8. If someone believes something that is *contrary* to what you believe, do you agree with him or her? Explain.

_____

_____

School–Home Connection
Ask your child to write one question and answer using each Vocabulary Word.

165

Practice Book
© Harcourt • Grade 6

► Read the selection "Eager." Then fill in the chart with examples of the appropriate character traits and clues from the story.

Character and Character Trait	Clues from Story

► Write a summary of "Eager" on a separate sheet of paper.

▶ Read the story. In the chart, write Charlie's and Zozo's character traits. Then write clues from the story that reveal each character's traits.

When Charlie stepped outside his front door, his first thought was that it looked like an ordinary day. The sun was shining, the flowers were blooming, and the spaceship was parked in front of the house. He wondered if, as usual, he had forgotten something important for school that day. *Absentminded Charlie* is what his friends sometimes called him. And now, something seemed…

"Spaceship?! Did I see a spaceship parked in front of my house?" Charlie said.

There was indeed a spaceship, and coming out the door was a little green man. "My name is Zozo, and I am afraid I am lost. Could you help me find my way east?" He held out his hand hesitantly.

"Wow, sure, cool," said Charlie. "By the way, my name is Charlie." He held out his right hand.

"Good morning, Charlie," said Zozo as he shook Charlie's hand hesitantly. "I don't want you to be late for anything. If you show me the way east, I'll surely find my home."

Then Charlie had an idea. If he could get a picture of Zozo, the kids at school might call him *Charlie the Great* instead. He ran into the house for a camera.

Five minutes later, Charlie came back out. The street was empty. Zozo's spaceship was a dot in the sky. Charlie stared at it until it disappeared. Then he laughed.

"Serves me right," he said to himself. "If I just kept track of my things, I might be famous today."

Character and Character Traits	Clues from Story

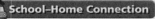
Practice Book
© Harcourt • Grade 6

▶ Fold the paper along the dotted line. As each Spelling Word is read aloud, write it in the blank. Then unfold your paper and check your work. Practice writing any Spelling Words you missed.

1. _____

2. _____

3. _____

4. _____

5. _____

6. _____

7. _____

8. _____

9. _____

10. _____

11. _____

12. _____

13. _____

14. _____

15. _____

16. _____

17. _____

18. _____

19. _____

20. _____

Spelling Words

1. ability
2. able
3. decompose
4. decomposition
5. familiar
6. family
7. muscle
8. muscular
9. meter
10. metric
11. precise
12. precision
13. relate
14. relative
15. commerce
16. commercial
17. similar
18. similarity
19. offense
20. offensive

School–Home Connection

Have your child write the Spelling Words on slips of paper. Play Go Fish and try to collect pairs of related words.

Spelling Practice Book
© Harcourt • Grade 6

Name _____

▶ Write the word in parentheses ( ) that correctly completes the sentence.

1. Visitors couldn't go _____ outside the viewing area. (nowhere, anywhere)

2. Nobody would _____ believe the things the robots could do. (ever, never)

3. The results hadn't been reported in _____ newspapers. (no, any)

4. No previous experiment _____ even come close to this. (had, hadn't)

▶ Use each adverb to write a sentence. Be certain to use the word as an adverb.

5. earliest

_____

6. carefully

_____

7. better

_____

8. farthest

_____

9. faster

_____

10. happily

_____

School–Home Connection

Ask your child to write three sentences about a school activity. Have your child include one of the following adverb forms in each sentence: positive, comparative, superlative.

169

► **Underline the sentence that best uses the Vocabulary Word.**

Sentence 1	Sentence 2
1. The *imposter* insisted he was the true prince.	At daybreak, we took a ride in the *imposter*.
2. I spoke very clearly to make sure there wouldn't be any *misapprehension*.	There was a *misapprehension*, so I was easily able to follow the directions.
3. The man was in a hurry and decided to *linger* a bit more before going.	Jake wanted to *linger* at the party even though it was way past his bedtime.
4. "I'm so glad you all came!" Marta said *dejectedly*.	"I miss my friends," Marta said *dejectedly*.
5. The evil king was *banished* from the kingdom and never seen again.	After I was *banished*, I came back to visit the next day.

► **Use what you know about the Vocabulary Words to answer the questions below. Write your answers in complete sentences.**

6. What can you do to get out of the *doldrums*?

_____

_____

7. What are some rules you must *abide* by at your school?

_____

_____

8. What is the most *strenuous* activity that you have recently done?

_____

_____

School–Home Connection

With your child, discuss the Vocabulary Word in each sentence. Have your child tell you the meaning in his or her own words.

170

▶ Read each section of "The Phantom Tollbooth." Write Milo's character traits as you read. Describe the story clues you used to identify the traits.

MILO	Character Traits	Clues from Story
Section 1 pages 748–752		
Section 2 pages 753–756		
Section 3 pages 757–759		
Section 4 pages 760–764		
Section 5 pages 765–767		
Section 6 pages 768–769		

► **Write a character trait for the underlined character name in each paragraph.**

1. Everyone was happy that <u>Raymond</u> had decided to come to the party. Raymond always told such good jokes and made a lot of people laugh.

   Character Trait: _____

2. "Are we almost there yet?" <u>Star</u> asked her father. They were on their way to visit Star's cousin, who lived an hour away. Star's father sighed. They had been driving for only fifteen minutes, and this was already the third time Star had asked that question.

   Character Trait: _____

3. <u>Martha</u> looked around her room. It was a mess. It would take way too much time to put everything away. Martha would much rather just plunk herself down in front of the TV and watch her favorite show.

   Character Trait: _____

4. <u>Rose</u> stood at the edge of the high-dive board. Secretly she was afraid of diving from so high up. But if she wanted to be part of the swim team, she had to overcome her fear and just do it. Rose waved to her coach and took a deep breath. Then she got into position, gave a bounce, and dove toward the cold, blue water.

   Character Trait: _____

5. <u>Isaac</u> put the bag of candy under his shirt. No one would see it there. Isaac's brother was in the living room reading. Isaac carefully sneaked past the living room and went quietly upstairs to his own room. No one saw him, which was good because he had no intention of sharing the candy with his brother. Isaac happily dumped the bag on his bed and began sorting out all the different kinds of candy.

   Character Trait: _____

School–Home Connection

Have a discussion with your child about a favorite character from a book, play, or movie. Discuss the traits of the character. Talk about the story clues that reveal those traits.

172

Practice Book
© Harcourt • Grade 6

Name _____

▶ Fold the paper along the dotted line. As each Spelling Word
is read aloud, write it in the blank. Then unfold your paper
and check your work. Practice writing any Spelling Words
you missed.

1. _____
2. _____
3. _____
4. _____
5. _____
6. _____
7. _____
8. _____
9. _____
10. _____
11. _____
12. _____
13. _____
14. _____
15. _____
16. _____
17. _____
18. _____
19. _____
20. _____

Spelling Words

1. allergies
2. data
3. bacteria
4. yourselves
5. potatoes
6. pianos
7. loaves
8. canoes
9. thieves
10. scarves
11. chiefs
12. lenses
13. quizzes
14. heroes
15. oxen
16. batteries
17. mosquitoes
18. spacecraft
19. crises
20. vetoes

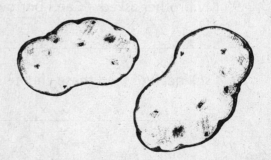

School–Home Connection

Have your child write ten sentences using all
the Spelling Words. Check to be sure they used
the words correctly.

173

Name _____

▶ **Add the correct punctuation mark where it belongs in each sentence.**

1. Grandma said, It's a long trip, so take several books to read."

2. "I'll take the book about the adventures of a boy named Milo, said Lisa.

3. Milo meets the following characters Tock, King Azaz, and the Mathemagician.

▶ **Read each sentence. If capitalization and punctuation are used correctly, write** *correct.* **If they are not, rewrite the sentence correctly.**

4. "Because the words are long said Ms. Jackson, you'll need to study hard.

   _____

5. "These are the subjects we'll cover: spelling, grammar, and word choice," she said.

   _____

6. Be sure to take plenty of notes during the lecture Dave said.

   _____

7. "Terry said if you run out of paper, let me know."

   _____

8. While we'll try to take breaks Grandma mentioned "We'll study many long hours."

   _____

   _____

9. My brother asked, "Can I borrow your book, Lisa?"

   _____

10. I still need to read these chapters: one, five, and seven, said Lisa.

   _____

School–Home Connection

Have your child use quotation marks while
writing four sentences that tell about a
conversation that took place at school today.

174

Name _____

► Underline the sentence that best uses the Vocabulary Word.

Sentence 1	Sentence 2
1. If I had something special, I would only *entrust* it to someone I knew.	If I had something special, I would only *entrust* it to a stranger.
2. Finding the right color socks was *critical* for us.	Finding the right path home was *critical* for us.
3. It was an *understatement* to say the flooding river made us nervous.	It was an *understatement* to say the flooding river made us happy.
4. The boy's soft whisper *emanates* from the alley.	The boy's drum playing *emanates* from the alley.
5. A wild animal's *erratic* behavior might mean it is healthy.	A wild animal's *erratic* behavior might mean it is ill.
6. Because the sun was so *elusive*, we canceled the day at the beach.	Because the sun was so *elusive*, we knew we would get a sunburn.
7. The Wright brothers' first flight at Kitty Hawk was an *unprecedented* act.	The regular flight from New York to Chicago is an *unprecedented* act.
8. My ears were not used to the *cacophony* of sounds coming from the sky.	My eyes were not used to the *cacophony* of sights coming from the sky.
9. When the house *imploded*, it caused much damage to the nearby houses.	When the house *imploded*, it caused little damage to the nearby houses.
10. Because Jan's pain was *acute*, we paid no attention to it.	Because Jan's pain was *acute*, we rushed her to the hospital.

School–Home Connection

Have your child read the sentences above.
Then ask your child to make up two sentences
for each word — one using it correctly and one
using it incorrectly. Discuss what makes the
sentences right or wrong.

Practice Book
© Harcourt • Grade 6

▶ Read the passage below and then fill in the Evidence and
Conclusion boxes.

Dirty Snowballs in the Sky

Comets are sometimes called "dirty snowballs" or "icy mudballs."
This is because they are made up of water and frozen gas that has mixed
with cosmic dust to form a small celestial body with a very long tail. The
tail is called a dust tail and can be 10 million kilometers long! The dust tail is what we can
see from Earth.

One feature of comets is that they have orbits. Orbits are the paths the comets take
as they travel around the sun. Of the approximately 878 comets that astronomers have
cataloged, about 184 are called periodic comets. This means they can be seen from Earth
more than once every 200 years. The most famous of these comets is Halley's Comet,
which was first documented by the Chinese in 240 B.C. It was named after Edmund Halley,
the scientist who predicted the comet's 76-year orbit.

Many of the the other comets' orbits take them deep into space. Even when we can't
see them, it is fun to think they are up there, their long tails sparkling in the sunlight.

Evidence	Conclusion

School–Home Connection

Your child is reviewing how to draw and
evaluate conclusions. With your child, watch
a program for children about science on
television. Help your child take notes on the
program and discuss its conclusions.

▶ Read the two passages below. Put a checkmark by the passage that you feel gives you a better description of the character. Then write a short description of the character on the lines provided.

> ## AUNT MINNIE
>
> Aunt Minnie is my aunt. I like her very much. She looks pretty normal and I guess she is. She loves me and is always nice to me. This makes me feel special around her. My mom likes her, too, and even my cat likes to sit on her lap.

> ## AUNT MINNIE
>
> I always hear my Aunt Minnie before I see her. She has a big booming laugh, which is surprising because she is a tiny person. Tiny, but full of OOMPH, my mom says. When she comes into view, she gives me the high-five sign, and then a big hug follows. Those hugs make me feel like the most special person in the world. Next she asks where Gruffy, my cat, is. She knows that next to her, I love Gruffy almost more than anything in the world.

_____

_____

_____

_____

School–Home Connection

Your child is reviewing characterization this week. With your child, think of a person you both know. Write down that person's character traits. Then, using the traits, help your child write a short character study of that person.

Name _____

▶ **Read the following sentences and identify whether they are fact or opinion. On the lines provided, tell why you feel the statement is a fact or an opinion.**

1. The sun is our nearest star. _____

   _____

2. We should work to save the Earth's endangered animals. _____

   _____

   _____

3. Going up in a hot-air balloon is always dangerous. _____

   _____

4. Poison ivy causes welts and itching on many people's skin. _____

   _____

5. You don't want to get poison ivy! _____

   _____

6. People ought to get more sleep. _____

   _____

7. Some doctors say to drink eight glasses of water a day. _____

   _____

8. Comets are made up of frozen gases and water and cosmic dust. _____

   _____

School–Home Connection

Your child is reviewing fact and opinion. Take a
walk with your child. Together, observe what is
around you, and make a factual statement and
then an opinion statement about each thing
you see.

178

▶ Read the following poem and think about each underlined word. If the word is used to mean its dictionary definition, write *denotation* on the line provided. If the word is used to create emotions and images, write what images the word brings to mind.

Shimmering Chimneys

We heard a tale of <u>shimmering</u> chimneys **beauty, sparkly, light** _____

of <u>gold</u> and <u>silver</u>, <u>copper</u> and <u>zinc</u>, **denotation** _____

diamonds even

buried deep under the <u>placid</u> <u>turquoise</u> waters **quiet, uneventful; beautiful** _____

in the sea off Japan.

<u>Volcanoes</u>, we were told, _____

hundreds, maybe even thousands of them,

<u>spouting</u> <u>fishtails</u> of precious metals and gems _____

in lines on the sea floor.

The metals settle in <u>mounds</u>. _____

The mounds grow, year after century.

Some have seen these <u>chimneys</u>. _____

Some have come back to tell of their <u>splendor</u>. _____

I can only <u>gaze</u> at the clear water. _____

No matter how far down I look,

It isn't far enough.

School–Home Connection

Your child is learning about connotation and denotation. Read some poems with your child and discuss which words express denotation and which express connotation.

179

► Fold the paper along the dotted line. As each Spelling Word is read aloud, write it in the blank. Then unfold your paper and check your work. Practice writing any Spelling Words you missed.

1. _____

2. _____

3. _____

4. _____

5. _____

6. _____

7. _____

8. _____

9. _____

10. _____

11. _____

12. _____

13. _____

14. _____

15. _____

16. _____

17. _____

18. _____

19. _____

20. _____

Spelling Words

1. postponement
2. uncertainly
3. unexpectedly
4. microscope
5. aquatic
6. rhythm
7. plumber
8. reign
9. soften
10. wrinkled
11. muscle
12. muscular
13. precise
14. precision
15. offense
16. offensive
17. pianos
18. canoes
19. chiefs
20. oxen

Practice Book
© Harcourt • Grade 6

▶ Read this part of a student's rough draft. Then answer the
questions that follow.

> (1) Sulima and Jon <u>were studying</u> deep-sea diving last year. (2) "<u>Their</u> the best divers in the class," the instructor told the coach. (3) The instructor said, "Next year, <u>I</u> be checking to see if they are still diving in these waters." (4) Then the instructor told Sulima and Jon, "<u>I am looking</u> for divers now to help with the big coral dive. (5) The job is <u>yours</u>, if <u>your</u> interested. (6) _____ you please agree to make the dive?"

1. Which change, if any, should be made to the underlined words in Sentence 1?
   A is studying
   B will be studying
   C are studying
   D Make no change.

2. Which is the correct way to write the underlined word in Sentence 2?
   A There
   B They're
   C Their'
   D The'yre

3. Which change, if any, should be made to the underlined word in Sentence 3?
   A I'll
   B ll'l
   C I've
   D I'm

4. Which describes the underlined verb in Sentence 4?
   A present-progressive form
   B past-progressive form
   C future-progressive form
   D infinitive

5. Which change should the student make to Sentence 5?
   A Change *yours* to *you'rs*.
   B Change *yours* to *your's*.
   C Change *your* to *you're*.
   D Change *your* to *youre*.

6. Which could complete Sentence 6?
   A Wont
   B Won't
   C Wont'
   D Wo'nt

▶ Read this part of a student's rough draft. Then answer the
questions that follow.

(1) I had never seen nothing so beautiful as the boat. (2) "Because you have
been interested in sailing for such a long time," my aunt said, we are going sailing."
(3) I couldn't hardly believe my luck! (4) "I am so glad you are happy" my aunt said.
(5) "Before you board, be sure you are carrying the following life jacket,
sunglasses, sunscreen, and your camera." (6) I got on the boat _____.

1. Which change, if any, should be
   made to Sentence 1?
   A Change *never* to *ever*.
   B Change *nothing* to *anything*.
   C Change *had never* to *hadn't never*.
   D Change *had never* to *haven't ever*.

2. Which change should the student
   make to Sentence 2?
   A Remove the quotation mark
      before the word *Because*.
   B Remove the comma after the
      word *time*.
   C Add a quotation mark before the
      word *we*.
   D Add a comma after the word *are*.

3. Which is the correct way to write
   Sentence 3?
   A I could not hardly believe my luck!
   B I couldn't never believe my luck!
   C I could hardly believe my luck!
   D I could hardly not believe my luck!

4. Which punctuation mark is missing
   from Sentence 4?
   A colon
   B semicolon
   C comma
   D quotation mark

5. Which punctuation mark is missing
   from Sentence 5?
   A colon
   B semicolon
   C comma
   D quotation marks

6. Which word or words could complete
   Sentence 6?
   A eager
   B more eager
   C more eagerly
   D eagerly

Index

184

VOCABULARY

Practice Book
© Harcourt • Grade 6